Hiking
the
Beartooths

by
Bill Schneider

(Formerly *The Trail Guide to the Beartooths*)

**With Up-to-Date Fishing Information
by Rich Stiff, High Lakes Survey Coordinator
for the Montana Department of Fish, Wildlife & Parks**

FALCON™

Falcon Press® Publishing Co., Inc.,
Helena, Montana

A FALCON GUIDE

Falcon Press is continually expanding its list of recreational guidebooks. All books include detailed descriptions, accurate maps, and all the information necessary for enjoyable trips. You can order extra copies of this book and get information and prices for other Falcon guidebooks by writing Falcon Press, P.O. Box 1718, Helena, MT 59624 or by calling toll-free 1-800-582-2665. Also, please ask for a free copy of our current catalog.

All black-and-white photos by author unless noted otherwise.
Cover photo by Michael S. Sample

Library of Congress Cataloging-in-Publication Data

Schneider, Bill.
   Hiking the Beartooths / by Bill Schneider.
      p.   cm.
   Rev. ed. of: The trail guide to the Beartooths. c.1995.
   "A Falcon guide"—T.p. verso.
   ISBN 1-56044-427-4 (pbk.)
   1. Hiking—Beartooth Mountains (Mont. and Wyo.)—Guidebooks.
2. Backpacking—Beartooth Mountains (Mont. and Wyo.)—Guidebooks.
3. Fishing—Beartooth Mountains (Mont. and Wyo.)—Guidebooks.
4. Beartooth Mountains (Mont. and Wyo.)—Guidebooks. I. Schneider,
Bill. Trail guide to the Beartooths. II. Title.
GV199.42.M92B437 1996
796.5'1'786—dc20a   96-18383
                                                       CIP

 Text pages printed on recycled paper

CAUTION

   Outdoor recreational activities are by their very nature potentially hazardous. All participants in such activities must assume the responsibility for their own actions and safety. The information contained in this guidebook cannot replace sound judgment and good decision-making skills, which help reduce risk exposure, nor does the scope of this book allow for disclosure of all the potential hazards and risks involved in such activities.

   Learn as much as possible about the outdoor recreational activities you participate in, prepare for the unexpected, and be safe and cautious. The reward will be a safer and more enjoyable experience.

ACKNOWLEDGMENTS

No book, especially a trail guide, gets into print without lots of help. In this case, I received invaluable help from many people.

First, I must thank my hiking partners, Mike Cannon and Jim Melstad, who survived some major "power hiking" to cover those last miles before the snow fell in 1994, and my family who not only spent some long days on the trail with me but withstood many nights away from home, tight schedules, and the long process of writing the book on nights and weekends.

I also gathered vital information from other hikers—Ann Boyd, Cathy Wright, Dick Krott, and Mike Sample. And as you can see, Mike also provided many of the photos for the book.

My friends in the Forest Service (Tom Alt, Frank Cifala, Dan Tyers, and Lyle Hancock) helped me gather all those details and reviewed the draft manuscript. I also learned so much during those long talks on the trail with wilderness rangers Dorothy Houser and Susan Nicholas.

And of course, I owe a big thank you to my staff at Falcon, who endured my distraction with the book and helped me in a thousand ways to make it happen—especially Randall Green, our guidebook editor, Will Harmon, who edited the manuscript, and graphic artists Eric West and Chris Stamper, who did the maps and charts.

CONTENTS

Hiking above treeline on the Beartooth Plateau. Michael S. Sample photo.

MAP LEGEND

These symbols are used on maps throughout this book.

▓ ✕ ▓ ✤ ∶	Wilderness/National Park Boundary
▬▬▬▬▬	Paved Road
≡≡≡	Interstate Highway
= = = = = = ∶	Jeep Road
═══════	Dirt/Gravel Road
───────	Creek
⋙⋙⋙⋙	National Forest Boundary
─── ∙	State Boundary
▬▬▬▬	Rivers
▬ ▬ ▬ ▬ ∣	Described Trail
─ ─ ─ ─	Other Trail
∙∙∙∙∙∙∙∙∙	Other Route
⬭	Glacier
▓	Country Above 3500' Elevation
⬭	Lake
x⁷⁵²⁴	Mountain Peak
∧	Campsite
⟡	Ranger Station
⟩ᵣ	Pass/Saddle
▪	Building
178	Forest Road
○	Trailhead
④	State Road
②	US Highway
= = ∶⟨ = = ∶	Permanently Locked Gate
= = ∶⟨ = = ∶	Seasonally Locked Gate
⟡	Spring
⚒	Mine
◉	Point of Interest

THE TRAILHEADS

1. Boulder River
2. West Stillwater
3. Stillwater River
4. West Rosebud
5. East Rosebud
6. West Fork of Rock Creek
7. Lake Fork of Rock Creek
8. Rock Creek

9. Island Lake
10. Beartooth Lake
11. Clay Butte
12. Muddy Creek
13. Crazy Creek
14. Clarks Fork
    of the Yellowstone
15. Fisher Creek
16. Lake Abundance

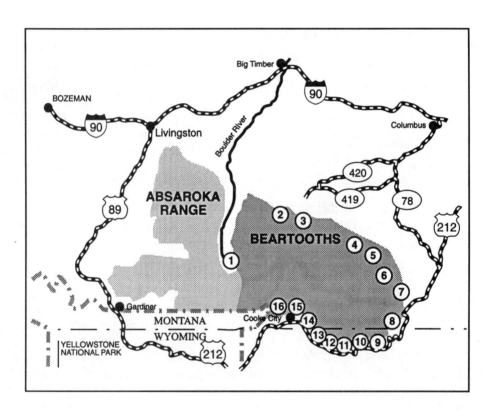

INTRODUCTION

The Beartooths aren't a national park. Even better. They are a national treasure.

This trail guide outlines trips of varying lengths, including day hikes and short, overnight trips. But most people quickly discover that a day or two in the Beartooths just isn't enough. Actually, it's probably impossible to get enough of the Beartooths.

The 943,377-acre Absaroka-Beartooth Wilderness is one of the most visited wilderness area in the United States. This is surprising considering snow covers the area until July and often comes again in early September. This book covers about two-thirds of the wilderness, the high-elevation, lake-strewn uplift, commonly called the Beartooth Plateau, or more simply, the Beartooths.

Even though the Beartooths attract lots of visitors, the area can absorb this use in a way that gives most everybody the feeling that they have the wilderness to themselves. Instead of competing for designated campsites or huts, backcountry travelers can camp anywhere. And anywhere is a big place in the Beartooths.

Almost all use in the Beartooths occurs between July 15 and September 15. During July and September, however, trails may be covered in snow, so most use is concentrated during a five-week period from the last week in July to the end of August. These facts conjure up images of crowded trails and overused campsites, but this rarely happens in the Beartooths.

Most people admire the Beartooths for their sheer, unbridled beauty. But many geologists marvel at this range for a different reason. A band of igneous rock rich in rare minerals lies along the northern edge of these mountains. The uplifted granite that comprises most of the range dates back more than three billion years and contains some of the oldest rocks on earth.

The Beartooths boast the highest mountain in Montana, Granite Peak, at 12,799 feet. From the top of Granite or many other peaks in the range, the view is dizzying.

With 944 lakes and nine major drainages, the Beartooths are also an angler's paradise. Rainbow, cutthroat, brook, golden, and lake trout thrive in the waterways of the plateau. Though the area is extremely popular, a persistent angler can usually find an unoccupied lake or stream to call his or her own for a day or two.

Much of the Beartooth Plateau rests at more than 10,000 feet, and is covered with delicate alpine tundra. Because of the high use, no-trace camping practices are essential to the preservation of this fragile ecosystem. Actually, most people visiting the Beartooths nowadays take great care to leave no trace of their visit. This is, of course, one reason this great masterpiece of the national forest system still seems pristine and uncrowded. It's the responsibility of all future visitors to carry on this tradition.

USING THIS GUIDEBOOK

This guidebook won't answer every question you have concerning your planned excursions into the Beartooths. But then, most people don't want to know everything before they go, lest they remove the thrill of making their own discoveries while exploring this magnificent wilderness. This book does provide the basic information needed to plan a successful trip.

TYPE OF TRIPS

Loop: Starts and finishes at the same trailhead, with very little retracing of your steps.

Shuttle: A point-to-point trip that requires two vehicles or an arrangement to be picked up at a designated time. The best way to manage the logistical problems of shuttles is to arrange for another party to start at the other end of the trail, meet in the middle and trade keys, and when finished, drive each other's vehicles home.

Out-and-Back: Traveling to a specific destination such as a lake or mountain top and then retracing your steps back to the trailhead.

Base Camp: An out-and-back trip involving a multi-night stay to enjoy short day trips from a base camp.

DISTANCES

It's almost impossible to get precisely accurate distances on trails. The distances used in this guidebook are based on a combination of actual experience hiking the trails, distances stated on Forest Service signs, and estimates from topo maps. In some cases, distances may be slightly off, so consider this when planning a trip. Keep in mind that distance is often less important than difficulty—a rough, 2-mile cross-country trek can take longer than 5 or 6 miles on a good trail.

RATINGS

The estimates of difficulty should serve as a general guide only, not the final word. What is difficult to one person may be easy to the next. In this guidebook, difficulty ratings take into account both how long and how strenuous the route is. Here are general definitions of the ratings.

Easy: Suitable for any hiker, including small children or the elderly, without serious elevation gain, no off-trail or hazardous sections, and no places where the trail is faint.

Moderate: Suitable for hikers who have some experience and at least an average fitness level, probably not suitable for small children or the elderly unless they have above-average level of fitness, perhaps with some short sections where the trail is difficult to follow, and often with some big hills to climb.

Difficult: Suitable for experienced hikers with above-average fitness level, often with some sections of the trail that are difficult to follow or some off-trail sections that could require knowledge of route-finding with topo map and compass, often with serious elevation gain, and possibly some hazardous conditions such as difficult stream crossings, snowfields, or cliffs.

In a few sidebars, the ratings have a more colorful definition of "human, semi-human, and animal." These ratings roughly equal the definitions of "easy, moderate, and difficult," although the "animal" rating would be described as "very difficult."

In addition to these ratings, many of the trail descriptions include a brief description of "special attractions" in the at-a-glance information. Make no mistake, there isn't a trail in the Beartooths that isn't special and incredibly scenic. But a handful of trails feature outstanding or unique natural qualities. These are highlighted here for easy reference.

SPECIAL REGULATIONS

The Forest Service has special regulations for hikers and backcountry horsemen. In some cases, the regulations apply throughout the Beartooths, while in other cases they apply to specific trails or ranger districts. Check with the Forest Service before you leave on your trip, and be sure to read and follow any special regulations posted at the trailhead. The Forest Service doesn't come up with these regulations to inconvenience backcountry visitors. Instead, they are designed to promote sharing and preservation of the wilderness.

INCONSISTENT NAMES

Some names of places and features used in this guidebook may not match the names found on some maps and in other books. In some cases, lakes named in this book are unnamed on some maps. The USGS maps, for example, list only officially approved names, but many lakes, streams, and mountains have common names that appear on other maps and in guidebooks, including, in some cases, this book.

KEY POINTS

A list of key points—stream crossings, trail junctions, notable landmarks, etc.—is provided for most of the trails described in this book. A few short trails, however, have no significant features along the way except the trailhead and destination. For these trails, no list of key points is given.

TRAILS ONLY

As mentioned several times in this guidebook, off-trail travel is the essence of the Beartooths. However, this guidebook does not, with a few exceptions, cover off-trail travel. Even those exceptions are cases where there has been so much off-trail travel on a certain unofficial route that the result has been a definable trail. Off-trail travel should be tried only after you've gained enough experience to feel confident with your abilities. Perhaps the best way to achieve this experience is to go on a few trips with an experienced off-trail hiker.

FOLLOWING FAINT TRAILS

Beartooth trails that receive infrequent use often fade away in grassy meadows, on ridges, or through rocky sections. Don't panic. These sections are usually short, and you can look ahead to see where the trail goes. Often the trail is visible going up a hill or through a hallway of trees ahead. If so, focus on that landmark and don't worry about not being off the trail for a short distance.

Also watch for other indicators that you are indeed on the right route, even if the trail isn't clearly visible. Watch for cairns, blazes, downfall cut with saws, and trees with the branches whacked off on one side. Follow only official Forest Service blazes, which are shaped like an upside-down exclamation point, and don't follow blazes made by hunters, outfitters, or other hikers to mark the way to some special spot.

SHARING

We all want our own wilderness area all to ourselves, but that happens only in our dreams. Lots of people use the Beartooths, and to make everyone's experience better we all must work at politely sharing the wilderness.

For example, hikers must share trails with backcountry horsemen. Both groups have every right to be on the trail, so please do not let it become a confrontation. Keep in mind that horses and mules are much less maneuverable than hikers, so it becomes the hiker's responsibility to yield the right-of-way. All hikers should stand on the downhill side of the trail, well off-trail for safety's sake, and let the stock quietly pass.

Another example of politely sharing the wilderness is choosing your campsite. If you get to a popular lake late in the day and all the good campsites are taken, don't crowd in on another camper. This is most aggravating, as these sites rightfully go on a first-come, first-served basis. If you're late, you have the responsibility to move on or take a less desirable site a respectable distance away from other campers.

FINDING MAPS

Good maps are easy to find, and they are essential to any wilderness trip. For safety reasons, maps are essential for route-finding and for "staying found." For non-safety reasons, most people would not want to miss out on the unending joy of mindlessly whiling away untold hours staring at a topo map and wondering what the world looks like here and there.

For trips into the Beartooths, there are three good choices for maps:

1. U.S. Geological Survey (USGS) topo maps.
2. An excellent Absaroka-Beartooth Wilderness map published by the USDA Forest Service.
3. A series of four hiking maps published by Rocky Mountain Survey (RMS), a private company in Billings, Montana.

In addition, ranger district maps are available from the various Forest Service offices in the region. The large wilderness map, however, more than meets any needs for Forest Service maps.

Which maps do you need? The well-prepared wilderness traveler will take all three. Look for maps at the following locations:

USGS: Check sporting goods stores in the Beartooth area or write directly to the USGS at the following address:

> Map Distribution
> U.S. Geological Survey
> Box 25286, Federal Center
> Denver, CO 80225

To make sure you order the correct USGS map, refer to the following grid.

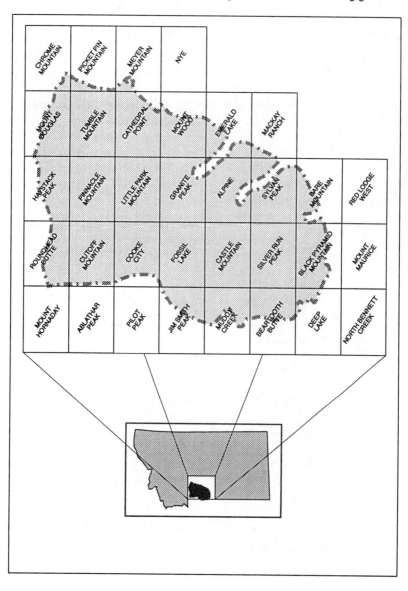

Forest Service: The Absaroka-Beartooth Wilderness map is also available at sporting good stores around the Beartooths, or call, stop by, or write to any of these Forest Service offices:

Custer National Forest   Phone: 406-657-6361
Forest Supervisor's Office
2602 First Avenue South
P.O. Box 2556
Billings, MT 59103

Gallatin National Forest   Phone: 406-587-6701
Forest Supervisor's Office
P.O. Box 130, Federal Building
Bozeman, MT 59715

Shoshone National Forest   Phone: 307-527-6241
Forest Supervisor's Office
808 Meadow Lane
Cody, WY 82414

RMS: Again, look for RMS maps at sporting goods stores in the Beartooth area, or write to:

Rocky Mountain Survey
P.O. Box 21558
Billings, MT 59104

FOR MORE INFORMATION

The best sources for more information on the Beartooths are the Forest Service ranger district offices. Unfortunately, this wilderness is managed by four different ranger districts and the exact areas of management are slightly confusing. Also, some trails go from one ranger district to another. The best approach is to contact the ranger district closest to the trailhead you intend to use.

Call or write the ranger districts at the following addresses:

Beartooth Ranger District   Phone: 406-446-2103
Custer National Forest
HC49, Box 3420
Red Lodge, MT 59068

Big Timber Ranger District   Phone: 406-932-5155
Gallatin National Forest
P.O. Box 196
Big Timber, MT 59011

Gardiner Ranger District   Phone: 406-848-7375
Gallatin National Forest
P.O. Box 5
Gardiner, MT 59030

Clarks Fork Ranger District   Phone: 307-754-2407
Shoshone National Forest
1002 Road 11
Powell, WY 82435

VACATION PLANNER

ADVENTURES, 4-7 NIGHTS

Base camps:
- Lake Plateau North
- Martin Lake
- Aero Lakes

Loops:
- Lake Plateau West
- Columbine Pass
- Green Lake
- Copeland Lake
- Lake Abundance

Shuttles:
- Slough Creek Divide
- Stillwater to Stillwater
- The Complete Stillwater
- The Beaten Path
- Rock Creek to Rock Creek
- Jorden Lake

SERIOUS, BUT NOT TOO SERIOUS, 1-3 NIGHTS

Base camps:
- Island Lake
- Quinnebaugh Meadows
- Becker Lake
- Native Lake

Loops:
- Claw Lake

Out-and-back trips:
- Breakneck Park Meadows
- Lake Wilderness
- Granite Peak
- Sylvan Lake
- Timberline Lake
- Lake Mary
- Quinnebaugh Meadows

Shuttles:
- Rosebud to Rosebud
- Silver Run Plateau
- Beartooth High Lakes
- Crazy Lakes

- Becker Lake
- Upper Granite Lake
- Lower Granite Lake
- Ivy Lake
- Fox Lake
- Rock Island Lake
- Lady of the Lake

SERIOUS DAY TRIPS:

East Fork Boulder River
Breakneck Park Meadows
Rosebud to Rosebud
Sylvan Lake
Silver Run Plateau
Timberline Lake
Quinnebaugh Meadows
Fox Lake
Curl Lake

Lake Mary
Hellroaring Lakes
Beartooth High Lakes
Claw Lake Loop
Upper Granite Lake
Lower Granite Lake
Ivy Lake
Rock Island Lake

EASY DAY TRIPS:

Sioux Charley Lake
Mystic Lake
Slough Lake
Elk Lake
Basin Creek Lakes
Broadwater Lake

Glacier Lake
Becker Lake
Beauty Lake
Lake Vernon
Lady of the Lake

AUTHOR'S RECOMMENDATIONS

FOR THAT FIRST NIGHT IN THE WILDERNESS:

Mystic Lake
Basin Creek Lakes
Timberline Lake
Becker Lake

Beauty Lake
Claw Lake Loop
Lady of the Lake

FOR ANGLERS:

East Fork Boulder River
Lake Plateau West
Slough Creek Divide
Columbine Pass
Stillwater to Stillwater
Copeland Lake Loop

The Beaten Path
Glacier Lake
Hellroaring Lakes
Native Lake Base Camp
Green Lake Loop
Aero Lakes Base Camp

FOR PHOTOGRAPHERS:

Columbine Pass Loop
Silver Run Plateau
The Beaten Path
Rock Creek to Rock Creek
Glacier Lake

Green Lake Loop
Becker Lake
Martin Lake Base Camp
Beartooth High Lakes

FOR CLIMBERS:

Granite Peak
The Beaten Path

Lake Wilderness
Aero Lakes Base Camp

FOR PEOPLE REALLY SCARED OF BEARS:

Slough Lake
Rosebud to Rosebud
Sylvan Lake
Rock Creek to Rock Creek
Glacier Lake
Hellroaring Lakes

Beartooth High Lakes
Beauty Lake
Claw Lake Loop
Becker Lake
Native Lake Base Camp

FOR PEOPLE WHO LIKE BEARS:

East Fork Boulder River
Slough Creek Divide
Lake Abundance Creek

FOR PARENTS WITH SMALL CHILDREN WHO WANT A REALLY EASY DAY HIKE:

Sioux Charley Lake
Slough Lake
Elk Lake

Broadwater Lake
Beauty Lake
Lady of the Lake

FOR PEOPLE WHO LIKE LONG DAY HIKES:

Rosebud to Rosebud
Sylvan Lake
Quinnebaugh Meadows

Silver Run Plateau
Beartooth High Lakes
Claw Lake Loop

FOR PEOPLE WHO JUST CAN'T GET ENOUGH ADVENTURE, WHO ARE WILDERNESS WISE, WHO LIKE A VARIETY OF OFF-TRAIL SIDE TRIPS:

Slough Creek Divide
Stillwater to Stillwater
The Beaten Path
Rock Creek to Rock Creek
Martin Lake Base Camp

Green Lake Loop
Copeland Lake Loop
Aero Lakes Base Camp
Lake Abundance Loop

FOR TRAIL RUNNERS AND POWER HIKERS:

Breakneck Park Meadows
Rosebud to Rosebud
Sylvan Lake
Basin Creek Lakes
Timberline Lake
Lake Mary

Quinnebaugh Meadows
Silver Run Plateau
Rock Creek to Rock Creek
Beartooth High Lakes
Claw Lake Loop
Ivy Lake

FOR BACKCOUNTRY HORSEMEN:

Slough Creek Divide
The Complete Stillwater
Stillwater to Stillwater
Jorden Lake
Copeland Lake Loop

Crazy Lakes
Breakneck Park Meadows
Quinnebaugh Meadows
Lower Granite Lake

Driving the Beartooth Highway—getting to the trailhead can be more exciting and scenic than the trip itself. Early users called the new road "no blushing maiden." Michael S. Sample photo.

LEAVE ONLY MEMORIES

Going into the Beartooths is like visiting a famous art museum. You obviously do not want to leave your mark on an art treasure in the museum. If everybody going through the museum left a little mark, the piece of art would be quickly destroyed. The same goes for a pristine wilderness, such as the Beartooths, which is as magnificent as any masterpiece of any artist.

The Beartooths have a large capacity for human use as long as everybody behaves. But a few thoughtless or uninformed visitors can ruin the wilderness for others. An important addition to the checklist is proper wilderness manners. Don't leave home without them.

All wilderness users have a responsibility to know and follow the rules of No-trace Camping. An important source of these guidelines, including the most updated research, can be found in the book, *Wild Country Companion*. Please see ordering information in the back of this book.

Nowadays most wilderness users want to walk softly, but some aren't aware that they have poor manners. Often their actions are dictated by the outdated understanding of a past generation of campers who cut green boughs for evening shelters and beds, built fire rings, and dug trenches around tents. In the 1950s, these "camping rules" may have been acceptable. But they leave long-lasting scars. Today such behavior is absolutely unacceptable. The wilderness is shrinking, and the number of users is mushrooming. More and more camping areas show unsightly signs of this trend.

Thus, a new code of ethics is growing out of necessity to cope with the unending waves of people wanting a perfect wilderness experience. Today we all must leave no clues that we have gone before. Canoeists can look behind them and see no trace of their passing. The same should be true of wild country recreation. Enjoy the wildness, but leave only memories behind.

Most of us know better than to litter—in or out of the wilderness. Be sure you leave nothing, regardless of how small it is, along the trail or at the campsite. This means you should pack out everything, including orange peels, flip tops, cigarette butts, and gum wrappers. Also pick up any trash that others leave behind.

Follow the main trail. Avoid cutting switchbacks and walking on vegetation beside the trail. In the Beartooths, some of the terrain is very fragile, so when going off-trail to get to a favorite lake or mountaintop, do your part not to create a new trail. And don't pick up "souvenirs," such as rocks, antlers, or wildflowers. The next person wants to see them, too.

Traditionally, backcountry trails are often marked by cairns or blazes. Cairns (small stacks of rocks) are commonly used to mark confusing places in official alpine trails, but avoid building cairns when traveling cross-country. They detract from the wilderness experience and can promote the repeated use of a specific route, eventually creating a new trail. Blazes, usually an upside-down exclamation point carved into the bark of trees, are found along many maintained wilderness trails, but individuals should never blaze trees in the backcountry.

Try to camp below timberline. Alpine areas are delicate and require special care.

Hiking along Rimrock Lake in the East Rosebud, one of the lower elevation trails in the Beartooths. Michael S. Sample photo.

Often it's only a short hike to a good campsite below timberline. When feasible, keep your camp away from a shoreline or stream bank, setting up the tent at least 200 feet from a lake or stream. And try to use established campsites so you won't cause additional damage by establishing a new one. When fetching water, use established paths or vary your route if there are none. Be sure to check at the trailhead for special regulations on camping and fire building which are in force in many places in the Beartooths and may change periodically.

Avoid making loud noises that may disturb others. Remember, sound travels easily to the other side of the lake. Be courteous.

Be very careful with food wastes to prevent unsightly messes and bad odors. Since almost all of the Beartooths is bear country, if you have a campfire, burn all food wastes. Throw cans and aluminum foil into the fire to burn off food scraps and odors. Then, before breaking camp, you must dig all cans and foil out of the ashes and pack them out. And be sure to pack out non-combustibles or unburned scraps from the fire pit thoughtlessly left by other campers.

Likewise, completely burn fish viscera. If fires aren't allowed, place fish viscera and leftover food in plastic bags and carry it out. Never throw fish viscera into mountain streams and lakes.

As noted in the chapter on bears, you must be careful with fish viscera so you don't create hazardous situations for yourself or others. If you're positive you are not in bear country, you can bury fish viscera at least 200 feet from lakes or streams. If there's any doubt in your mind, pack them out. And if you're uncertain about what to do or nervous about bears, release all your fish and eat the food you carried in.

Pour your waste water from boiling foods around the perimeter of your fire to keep it from spreading. This also protects natural vegetation. Wash dishes and clothing well away from streams and lakes. Pour dishwater in a small sump hole and cover when breaking camp. Never wash dishes in a mountain stream or lake. If you use soap, make sure it's biodegradable.

As with food waste, be careful with human wastes. If you use toilet paper, use white, unscented paper and bury it 6-8 inches along with human waste. Thoroughly bury human wastes to avoid any chance of bad odor or water pollution. This is a good reason to carry a lightweight trowel. Keep wastes at least 200 feet away from lakes and streams.

Campfires probably cause more damage to the backcountry than any other aspect of camping. Although campfires are allowed in most parts of the Beartooths, avoid building fires in alpine areas where the surface is fragile and wood is scarce.

If a campfire is appropriate for the campsite, dig out the native vegetation and topsoil and set it aside. Don't build a fire ring with rocks. When breaking camp douse the fire thoroughly, and after you're positive it's completely out, scatter the cold ashes, and replace the native soil and vegetation. Another acceptable method is to spread several inches of mineral soil or sand on a flat rock to avoid fire-scarring the rock. Later scatter or bury the ashes and expose the rock, which should still look natural.

Build fires away from trees to prevent damage to root systems. Keep fires small and widely disperse any partially burned wood. Don't make a mess tearing apart trees to get firewood. Standing dead trees often are homes to many wild animals. Gather smaller fallen branches to burn. Don't use a saw or ax on a tree and leave a lasting scar.

Take a bath by jumping into the water and then climb out and move away from the water to lather yourself. Rinse off by pouring pans of water over your body away from your water source. This allows soap to biodegrade quickly as it filters through the soil. Use only biodegradable soap.

The no-trace ethic also applies to backcountry horsemen who have the potential to do much more damage than an equal number of hikers. The Forest Service has an excellent free brochure called "Horse Sense" on the subject.

Finally, and perhaps most important, strictly follow the pack-in, pack-out rule. If you carry something into the backcountry, consume it, burn it, or carry it out.

Leave no trace—and put your ear to the ground in the wilderness and listen carefully. Thousands of people who will come behind you are thanking you for your courtesy and good sense.

HAVE A SAFE TRIP

The Scouts have been guided for decades by perhaps the best single piece of safety advice—Be Prepared! For starters, this means carrying survival and first-aid materials, proper clothing, compass, and topographic map—and knowing how to use them.

Perhaps the second-best advice is to tell somebody where you're going and when you plan to return. Pilots must file flight plans before every trip, and anybody venturing into a blank spot on the map should do the same. File your "flight plan" with a friend or relative before taking off.

Close behind your flight plan and being prepared with proper equipment is physical conditioning. Being fit not only makes wilderness travel more fun, it makes it safer.

To whet your appetite for more knowledge of wilderness safety and preparedness, here are a few basic tips.

• Check the weather forecast. Be careful not to get caught at high altitude by a snowstorm, and watch the cloud formations closely to avoid being stranded on a ridgeline during a lightning storm. Don't plan on travel during prolonged periods of cold weather.

• If you build a fire, you are responsible for keeping the fire under control at all times. If your campfire runs wild and starts a wildfire, you will be held accountable for the huge expense of fighting the fire and for any damage resulting from carelessness. Be extra careful if the fire danger is high. Check with the respective Forest Service office for more information on fire danger and restrictions. If there is a forest fire in an area, consider that area off limits to outdoor recreation.

• Avoid traveling alone in the wilderness.

• Never split up in the backcountry.

• Withstand the temptation to swim across a high mountain lake or large stream.

• Be wary of steep snowbanks with rocks or cliffs at the bottom.

• Know the preventive measures, symptoms, and treatment of hypothermia, the silent killer.

• Study basic survival and first aid before leaving home.

• Don't eat wild mushrooms or other plants unless you are positive of their identification.

• Before you leave find out as much as you can about the route, especially any potential hazards.

Clarks Fork Trailhead, one of the many scenic and well-maintained trailheads in the Beartooths.

• Don't exhaust yourself or weaker members of your party by traveling too far or too fast. Let the slowest person set the pace.

• Don't wait until you're confused to look at your maps. Follow them as you go along, from the moment you start moving up the trail, so you have a continual fix on your location.

• If you get lost, don't panic. Sit down and relax for a few minutes while you carefully check out your topo map and take a compass reading. Confidently plan your next move. It's often smart to retrace your steps back to familiar ground, even if it might make the trip longer. Lots of people become temporarily lost in the wilderness and survive—usually by calmly and rationally dealing with the situation.

• Be extra cautious when fording a large stream. Use sandals or remove your socks and put your boots back on. This makes for more secure footing on the slippery stream bottom. Avoid the current's full force by keeping sideways to the flow. Slide—don't lift—each foot one at a time, making sure that one foot is securely anchored before seeking a new hold with the other one. Go slowly and deliberately. If using a walking stick, keep it on the upstream side for additional support.

• Stay clear of all wild animals, and this goes triple for bears.

Last but not least, don't forget that the best defense against unexpected hazards is knowledge. Read up on the latest in wilderness safety information in the recently published book, *Wild Country Companion*. Check the back of this guidebook for ordering information.

SURVIVAL KIT

A survival kit should include: compass, whistle, matches in a waterproof container, cigarette lighter, candle, emergency fishing gear (sixty feet of six-pound line, six hooks, six lead shot, and six trout flies), signal mirror, fire starter, aluminum foil, water purification tablets, space blanket, and flare.

FIRST-AID KIT

A good first-aid kit should include: sewing needle, a snake-bite kit, aspirin, antibacterial ointment, two antiseptic swabs, two butterfly bandages, adhesive tape, four adhesive strips, four gauze pads, two triangular bandages, codeine tablets, two inflatable splints, moleskin, one roll of three-inch gauze, CPR shield, rubber gloves, and lightweight first-aid instructions.

THE SILENT KILLER

Be aware of the danger of hypothermia—a condition in which the body's internal temperature drops below normal. It can lead to mental and physical collapse and death.

Hypothermia is caused by exposure to cold, and it's aggravated by wetness, wind, and exhaustion. The moment you begin to lose heat faster than your body produces it, you're suffering from exposure. Your body starts involuntary exercise such as shivering to stay warm, and your body makes involuntary adjustments to preserve normal temperature in vital organs, restricting blood flow in the extremities. Both responses drain your energy reserves. The only way to stop the drain is to reduce the degree of exposure.

With full-blown hypothermia, your energy reserves are exhausted and cold reaches the brain, depriving you of good judgment and reasoning power. You won't be aware that this is happening. You lose control of your hands. Your internal temperature slides downward. Without treatment, this slide leads to stupor, collapse, and death.

To defend against hypothermia, stay dry. When clothes get wet, they lose about 90 percent of their insulating value. Wool loses relatively less heat; cotton, down, and some synthetics lose more. Choose raingear that covers the head, neck, body, and legs and provides good protection against wind-driven rain. Most hypothermia cases develop in air temperatures between 30 and 50 degrees Fahrenheit, but hypothermia can develop in warmer temperatures.

If your party is exposed to wind, cold, and wet, think hypothermia. Watch yourself and others for these symptoms: Uncontrollable fits of shivering; vague, slow, slurred speech; memory lapses; incoherence; immobile, fumbling hands; frequent stumbling or a lurching gait; drowsiness (to sleep is to die); apparent exhaustion; and inability to get up after a rest.

When a member of your party has hypothermia, he or she may deny any problem. Believe the symptoms, not the patient. Even mild symptoms demand treatment, as follows:

- Get the patient out of the wind and rain.

- Strip off all wet clothes.

- If the patient is only mildly impaired, give him or her warm drinks. Then put the patient in warm clothes and a warm sleeping bag. Place well-wrapped water bottles filled with heated water close to the patient.

- If the patient is badly impaired, attempt to keep him or her awake. Put the patient in a sleeping bag with another person—both naked. If you have a double bag, put two warm people in with the patient.

WOOD TICKS

Ticks are fairly common throughout wooded, brushy, and grassy areas, including those in the Beartooths. They are most active from March until early summer. All ticks are potential carriers of Rocky Mountain spotted fever, which can be transmitted when the tick bites and sucks a host's blood. The western black-legged tick is responsible for transmitting Lyme disease, a bacterial infection named for the Connecticut town where it was first recognized. These diseases are transmitted to humans and other mammals by the bite of an infected tick.

The best defense against hosting a tick is to avoid areas infested with ticks. If that's not always possible, wear clothing with a snug fit around the waist, wrists, and ankles. Layers of clothing are most effective in keeping ticks from reaching the body. And since ticks do not always bite right away (they often crawl around on a potential host for several hours before deciding where to feed), a strong insect repellent can also be an effective deterrent against tick bites.

LIGHTNING

Do not be caught on a ridge or a mountaintop, under large solitary trees, in the open, or near open water during a lightning storm. Try to seek shelter in a low-lying area, ideally in a dense stand of small, uniformly sized trees. Stay away from anything that might attract lightning, such as metal tent poles, graphite fishing rods, or pack frames.

YES, FORTUNATELY, THERE ARE BEARS

Because much of the Beartooths is open terrain and above timberline, some people infer that there couldn't be bears here. Wrong!

Backcountry travelers can run into a bear—black bear or grizzly—on any trip into the Beartooths, anytime, anywhere, so it's important to take the necessary precautions. No set of rules will guarantee complete wilderness safety. But this section contains the basic information necessary to make bear country as safe as possible.

In general: Be cautious and alert. Don't travel alone. Watch for bear sign and be extra careful if you find any. Leave your dog at home. Report all bear incidents to local authorities.

On the trail: Avoid surprising a bear—make noise. Metallic noise is much more effective than human voices. Metallic noise is only made by humans. Human voices can be muffled by natural conditions, and it's difficult to keep up steady conversation.

If you see a bear at a distance on or near the trail, you face a difficult decision. You may not want to disturb the bear at all, both out of concern for the bear and for yourself. This means abandoning your trip or at least backtracking a safe distance and waiting for a few hours until, with a little luck, the bear moves on.

If you decide to proceed, however, be extra cautious. Make a wide detour around the bear on its upwind side so that it can get your scent. If a detour is not possible, slowly back down the trail until safely out of the bear's sight. Then make lots of noise (the more, the better) and slowly make your way up the trail again. The bear should be gone when you get back to your earlier observation point. If the bear is still there and you can't safely get around it, abandon your route.

Makeshift, but still bearproof, evening food storage in the Beartooths.

In camp: Be careful with food and garbage. Keep a clean camp. Don't camp in a site obviously frequented by bears. If you see a bear or fresh sign where you intended to camp, pick another campsite. If possible, camp near tall trees that can easily be climbed. Sleep at least 100 yards from your campfire and cooking area. In bear country, always hang your food and garbage at night. Ideally, try for the "Three-Ten Rule"—hang your food 10 feet above the ground and suspended on a rope strung between two trees, 10 feet from either tree. This is not always possible at high-elevation campsites with small trees, but get as close as you can. Keep food odors off clothes, tents, and sleeping bags. Avoid fresh, perishable, or smelly foods such as bacon, lunch meat, sardines, etc. The smell of fish can attract bears, so don't clean fish near camp. If possible, completely burn fish entrails. Camping at popular fishing sites requires extra caution.

Completely burn combustible trash if regulations and natural conditions allow camp-fires. Burn cans and other incombustibles to remove odors. Then dig them out of the ashes and pack them out. Never bury trash in the backcountry. If you can carry it in, you can carry it out.

Special precautions for women: Some people recommend women stay out of bear country during menstrual periods. But to date there is no evidence that bears are attracted to menstrual odors more than any other odor, and no known attacks have been traced to menstruation as the cause. The simple fact that bears have a keen sense of smell does, however, suggest that women should take common sense pre-cautions when traveling in bear country. Keep yourself as clean and odor free as possible. Use pre-moistened, unscented cleaning towelettes, and use tampons instead of pads. Do not bury used tampons or pads. A bear could smell them and dig them up. Used tampons or pads will provide a small food "reward" and may attract bears to other women menstruating. If possible, completely burn used tampons, pads, and towelettes. If not possible, place them in double airtight bags and store them with other garbage away from bears. Both men and women should avoid using perfume, hair spray, deodorants, and other cosmetics. There is some evidence that bears are attracted and even infuriated by these scents.

The confrontation: If you take the above precautions, the chances of encounter-ing a bear are slim. But if all fails, the most important advice is "don't panic."

Remember that a bear will try to avoid contact with humans, so if you meet a bear along the trail the odds are good that it will turn and flee. But in the event of a human-bear confrontation, the best course of action is to talk in a firm, unexcited voice to the bear while slowly backing away. Do not attempt to run away from the bear as this may cause the bear to mistake you for prey and give chase. You can't outrun a bear. Climbing a tree is a means of escape if an appropriate tree is nearby and you have enough time to do so (which is usually not the case). Playing dead—curling into a ball face-down and covering the neck and stomach—should be used only as a last resort after the bear has decided to attack.

Publisher's note: Keep in mind these are merely general rules, but, as always, it's dan-gerous to generalize—and especially about bears. Certainly, there is no concrete formula for avoiding confrontations or for what to do when confronted. Every incident is differ-ent. And keep in mind that it's far easier to avoid a bear encounter than get out of one.

WATER, WATER EVERYWHERE, BUT NOT A DROP TO DRINK

Few backcountry pleasures can top a cool drink from a high-country lake or stream. That refreshing drink of water along the trail is almost a tradition. But now, like other grand old traditions, this one is fading away.

An abhorrent protozoan called *Giardia lamblia* has changed the way we drink. This single-celled microscopic parasite, now found throughout the Beartooths and most other wild areas, causes severe intestinal disease.

All wilderness users must now take appropriate measures to insure water is pure by taking one of the following steps:

• The best protection is to pack water from the faucet, but this is difficult for long trips.

• Boiling water for at least ten minutes is probably the surest way to kill *Giardia* and other water-borne microorganisms.

• Also, many types of water filters can purify water. These filters are probably the safest choice next to boiling.

• Another purification method involves adding tincture of iodine, a saturated solution of iodine, or other water purification tablets that are readily available at backpacking and sporting goods stores.

Also, be aware of the source of your water. Snow melt, springs, and small, intermittent streams are safer than large streams or lakes. Take water upstream from the trail.

One final note. If you become ill about two to four weeks after your backcountry visit, see a physician immediately.

Filtering water, strongly recommended for all waters in the Beartooths. Michael S. Sample photo.

THE BEARTOOTH FISHERY

By Richard K. Stiff
High Mountain Lakes Survey Coordinator
Montana Department of Fish, Wildlife and Parks

The Absaroka-Beartooth Wilderness contains about 944 lakes, and of these, 328 support fisheries and 616 are barren. Only a few lakes in the entire wilderness (within the Slough Creek drainage) are thought to contain native fish, with surviving original Yellowstone cutthroat stock. All other fisheries within the wilderness were created when fish were introduced to lakes or streams. In some cases, introduced fish migrated and established populations in new locations. Lakes are currently managed by drainage due to the nature of the drainages and fish migration within each drainage, although this has not always been the case.

More than sixty percent of the lakes within the wilderness are barren of fish, their natural condition. These provide an opportunity for backcountry travelers to get away from anglers and find more solitude. While most anglers would probably enjoy seeing fish in many of these lakes, leaving them in their natural state is a tribute to the Absaroka-Beartooth as a true "wilderness." Current laws prohibit the stocking of fish, without an environmental review, in lakes that have no history of a fishery. The distribution of lakes (with and without fish), by drainage is:

Boulder River	103
Clarks Fork	426
East Rosebud	76
Rock Creek	91
Slough Creek	10
Stillwater River	154
West Rosebud	84
TOTAL	944

The majority of the lakes are above 8,500 feet, with a number of these above 10,000 feet. Because of the high elevation, lakes often remain ice-covered until late June and have surface temperatures that seldom reach 60 degrees Fahrenheit. The size of the fish in a lake is generally related to the size of the population. There are usually a few large fish, many medium-sized fish, or lots of smaller fish.

Lakes that harbor self-sustaining populations of fish often tend to become over-populated, resulting in slower growth rates. Since brook trout have the least restrictive spawning requirements, they are most often the victims of poor growth rates. Lakes with brook trout tend to have stunted populations, although there are exceptions such as Cairn and Lower Aero lakes.

Many of the lakes managed within the wilderness do not have a suitable place for trout to spawn and must be stocked to maintain a fishery. Most stocked lakes are planted with fish on a rotating cycle of three, four, six, and eight years, depending on use and management goals. Knowing the year these lakes are stocked can increase an angler's chance of catching good fish. Three- to four-year old fish provide the best fishing for nice-sized trout.

Three- and four-year stocking cycles are generally used on lakes that receive significant fishing pressure and where a persistent good catch is desired. A six-year cycle allows at least some of the fish to grow larger, while still maintaining a constant fishery. Stocking at eight-year intervals is based on the premise that fish will live for seven years, and there will be a fallow year to allow the food population to recover. The eight-year cycle is used in lakes where a trophy-type fishery is desired, as well as in remote, relatively unproductive lakes. More lakes are being considered for the eight-year cycle.

There are many different species of fish in the Beartooths, although the majority of the lakes support only one species of fish. Cutthroat trout are the principal fish stocked because the area is in their original geographic range, and the hatchery in Big Timber provides an economical source of cutthroat trout. But many lakes were planted with brook trout in the first half of this century, and these have established populations.

Analysis of the fisheries reveals the following distribution of fish species:

➤ Arctic Grayling	11 lakes
Cutthroat Trout	117 lakes
Eastern Brook Trout	85 lakes
Golden Trout	25 lakes
Rainbow Trout	22 lakes
Mixed fishery	56 lakes
Undecided	12 lakes
TOTAL	328 lakes

Lake trout and brown trout are found in several mixed fisheries, mostly outside the wilderness boundaries.

Stream fisheries are different than lake fisheries. Since the Montana Department of Fish, Wildlife and Parks no longer plants fish in streams, the fish found there are self-supporting populations. Alpine streams, like alpine lakes, have a limited food supply. But in a stream the trout not only have to find food, they must also fight the current of the stream.

Trout rely on the current of the stream to bring food to them, while hiding from the current themselves. Places that do both of these things are at a premium, and the largest fish get the best spots. The number of good feeding spots and the amount of food available limit the number of fish that can be present in a given reach of stream. Streams tend to support fewer fish than lakes, but fish in streams are easier to locate. Anglers should note that stream and lake fishing regulations differ.

Trout can usually find suitable places to spawn in a stream, so reproduction is not a problem. The type of fish present usually reflects a combination of what was originally found in the stream, the fish that were planted, and the fish that have migrated down from lakes above.

One final note. The southeastern arm of the Beartooths straddles the border

Superb trout fishing complements the spectacular scenery of the Beartooths.

between Montana and Wyoming. Anglers in this area must be careful to fish only in the state for which they hold a valid fishing license. In some places, particularly where lakes actually straddle the border (as does Granite Lake, for example), it might be wise to carry licenses for both states. Also know and heed the appropriate regulations.

SUGGESTED EQUIPMENT LIST
FOR BACKPACKING THE BEARTOOTHS

Clothing: In general, strive for natural fibers such as cotton and wool and earth tones instead of neon colors. Dig around in the closet for something dull. Your wilderness partners will appreciate it.

Try out the clothing before leaving home to make sure everything fits loosely with no chafing. In particular, make sure your boots are broken in, lest they break you on the first day of the hike. Get good raingear. Weather in the Beartooths can be unpredictable, which means, of course, it can be very bad. You absolutely need high-quality raingear.

Also, pack enough clothes to keep you warm—regardless of how hot it is when you leave the trailhead or if the pack already seems too heavy. Leave something else home instead of warm clothes.

> Warm hat (i.e., stocking cap)
> Mittens or gloves
> Raingear
> Long underwear
> Water-resistant, windproof wilderness coat
> Heavy sweater and/or insulated vest
> Warm pants (i.e., sweat pants)
> Hiking shorts
> One pair of socks for each day, plus one extra pair of light hiking socks
>   and one extra pair of heavy wool socks
> Underwear
> Large-brimmed hat or cap
> Lightweight hiking boots
> Lightweight, long-sleeve shirts or t-shirts
> Short-sleeve shirts or t-shirts
> Sandals or lightweight shoes for fording streams and
>   wearing in camp

Hiking equipment: Equipment does not have to be new or fancy (or expensive), but make sure you test everything before you leave home.

> Tent and waterproof fly
> Sleeping bag (20 degrees F. or warmer) and stuff sack
> Sleeping pad
> Cooking pots and pot holder
> Water bottle
> Full-size backpack
> Day pack or fanny pack for day trips
> Cup, bowl, and eating utensils
> Lightweight camp stove and adequate fuel

Food: Bring enough food, including lots of high-energy snacks for lunching during the day, but don't overburden yourself with too much food. Plan meals carefully, bringing just enough food, plus some emergency rations. Avoid fresh, smelly foods and canned foods. Freeze-dried foods are the lightest and safest, but they are expensive and not really necessary. Don't forget hot and cold drinks.

Miscellaneous: (* - optional).

Garbage sacks
Small zip-lock bags
Stuff sacks*
Paper towels*
Nylon cord (50 feet)
Compass
Toilet trowel
Toilet paper*
Sun screen and lip lotion
First-aid kit
Binoculars*
Camera and extra film*

Flashlight and extra batteries
Pocket knife
Fishing equipment* and permits
Sunglasses
Insect repellent
Matches in waterproof container
Small towel
Personal toilet kit
Notebook and pencil*
Water filter or water purification tablets
Maps

One of the easiest stretches of the off-trail section between Crow Lake and Lake Mary.
Dick Krott photo.

TRAILHEAD 1
BOULDER RIVER

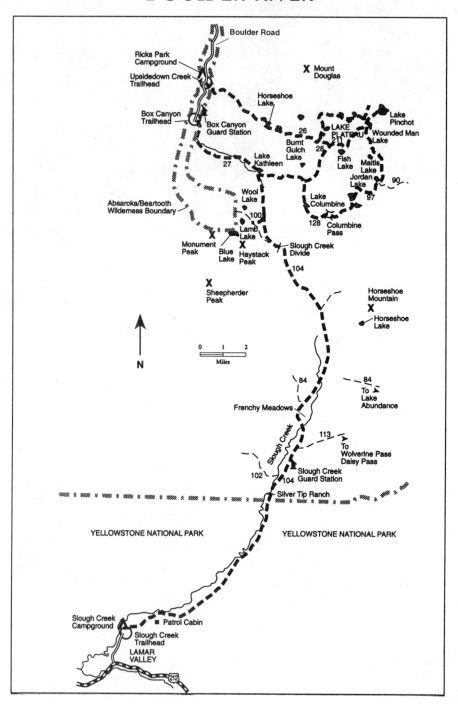

Boulder Road

Ricks Park
Campground

Upsidedown Creek
Trailhead

X Mount
Douglas

Box Canyon
Trailhead

Horseshoe
Lake

Box Canyon
Guard Station

Lake
Pinchot

LAKE
PLATEAU
211

Wounded Man
Lake

26

Burnt
Gulch
Lake

28

27

Lake
Kathleen

Fish
Lake

Maitis
Lake

Jordan
Lake

90

Wool
Lake

Lake
Columbine

97

Absaroka/Beartooth
Wilderness Boundary

100

128

Columbine
Pass

X
Monument
Peak

Lamb
Lake

X

Blue
Lake

Haystack
Peak

Slough Creek
Divide

104

X
Sheepherder
Peak

Horseshoe
Mountain

X
Horseshoe
Lake

0   1   2
Miles

N

84

84
To
Lake
Abundance

Frenchy Meadows

113
To
Wolverine Pass
Daisy Pass

Slough Creek

102

Slough Creek
Guard Station

104

Silver Tip Ranch

YELLOWSTONE NATIONAL PARK

YELLOWSTONE NATIONAL PARK

Slough Creek
Campground

Patrol Cabin

Slough Creek
Trailhead

LAMAR
VALLEY

212

OVERVIEW

Most locals consider the Boulder River the dividing line between the Beartooths to the east and the Absaroka Range to the west. This road and the long trip through Slough Creek also form the western boundary of the terrain covered in this trail guide.

The Boulder River Road ends 50 miles south of Big Timber at Box Canyon Campground. In the 1970s there was a proposal to punch the road all the way through to Cooke City, splitting the wilderness into two smaller wild areas. Look at a topo map and the feasibility of such a road becomes obvious. After a hard fight by wilderness advocates, the two spectacular mountain ranges were permanently joined into one wilderness, and the controversial road proposal was dropped.

The Boulder River is a popular place. The road is lined with dude ranches and church camps in addition to numerous summer homes. During the early hunting season in September as many as fifty or more horse trailers may be parked at Box Canyon Trailhead.

The Lake Plateau region of the Beartooths is as popular as any spot in the entire wilderness. The Boulder River trailheads (Box Canyon and Upsidedown Creek) attract many backpackers. Few backcountry horsemen use Upsidedown Creek, and many who use Box Canyon are hunters and outfitters going into Slough Creek.

The Lake Plateau is a unique and spectacular part of the Beartooths accessed by four major trails. Two of these trails (Lake Plateau West and Columbine Pass) originate along the Boulder River. Others leave from the West Stillwater (Lake Plateau North) and the main Stillwater (Lake Plateau East).

FINDING THE TRAILHEAD

To find the trailhead, take County Road 298 (locally referred to as the Boulder River Road) south from Big Timber. The road doesn't take off from either of the two exits off Interstate 90. Instead, go into Big Timber and watch for signs for County 298, which heads south and passes over the freeway from the middle of town between the two exits.

It's 48 miles from Big Timber to the Box Canyon Trailhead, so make sure to top off the gas tank. It's 16 miles to the small community of McLeod and 24 miles until the pavement ends—which, of course, means 24 miles of bumpy gravel road is still ahead. There are two major trailheads with parking areas (Upsidedown Creek and Box Canyon) providing access to the Lake Plateau and Slough Creek. Upsidedown Creek is about 1.5 miles before Box Canyon. Both trailheads are well signed.

A jeep road continues on to the Independence Peak area, where signs of early 1900s mining operations still remain. But almost all of the trails in this region can be accessed without bumping and grinding up this very rough road. At best it is passable only with four-wheel-drive or all-terrain vehicles.

East Fork Boulder River
Lake Plateau West
Columbine Pass Loop
Slough Creek Divide

1 EAST FORK BOULDER RIVER

General description: An easy day hike or overnighter.
Total distance: 7 miles.
Difficulty: Easy.
Special attractions: An easy hike along a beautiful stream with great fishing.
Topo maps: USGS—Mount Douglas and Haystack Peak; RMS— Mount Douglas-Mount Wood and Cooke City-Cutoff Mountain.

The trail: This trail is actually the "approach" to the popular routes into Lake Plateau and Slough Creek. Consequently, even though many people use this area, most of them hurry right through the East Fork Boulder River.

From the Box Canyon Trailhead, Trail 27 climbs gradually along the East Fork. The trail stays a fair distance from the river until about 3 miles in. The first part of this trail was once a wagon road, and it still looks like one. Fortunately, this

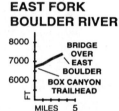

EAST FORK BOULDER RIVER

isn't because of heavy traffic, although the area receives fairly heavy use during July and August and again in September during the early hunting season.

The trail arrives at a great campsite about 3.5 miles from the trailhead and then crosses the East Fork on a well-constructed bridge. There is a large campsite here capable of handling a large party or several parties (stock users should check the Forest Service regulations for the area—including group size limits—when planning a trip here).

Day hikers can easily spend a few hours fishing or lounging around this area, and even those bound for higher regions will want to linger. The stream is as charming as they get, and the fishing is great. The bridge marks a good turn-around point for day hikers. Those with more time can continue east to where the trail forks, leading to extended trips up to Lake Plateau or south along Slough Creek.

> ➤ **Fishing information:** Above Box Canyon the East Fork Boulder River contains mostly cutthroat trout, although rainbows dominate the fishery below. Some of these cutthroats may be descendants of native stocks. A smattering of rainbows (immigrants from Rainbow Lakes above) can be found near where Rainbow Creek enters the East Fork Boulder River.

Cutthroat trout are aggressive and often easy to catch. As a result, where cutthroats dominate the fishery, fishing tends to be great. While this has been the fish's downfall in lower streams, most anglers in the Beartooths only keep enough for dinner, and populations seem to be stable.

None of the lakes near this route support a fishery. Lake Kathleen provides an opportunity to observe a lake in its natural, untarnished state.

2 LAKE PLATEAU WEST

General description:	A week-long backpacking vacation that can be done as a loop or an out-and-back.
Total distance:	22 to 28 miles depending on where you base camp.
Difficulty:	Moderate up Rainbow Creek; difficult up Upsidedown Creek.
Special attractions:	A gorgeous, lake-dotted, high-altitude plateau.
Topo maps:	USGS—Mount Douglas, Tumble Mountain, and Haystack Peak; RMS—Mount Douglas-Mount Wood and Cooke City-Cutoff Mountain.

Key points:

3.5	East Fork Boulder River.
5.2	Junction with Trail 28.
5.4	Lake Kathleen.
7.9	Junction with Trail 128.
10.5	Junction with Trail 211.
11.5	Junction with Trail 26.
12.3	Rainbow Lakes.
13.2	Wounded Man Lake.
14.0	Lake Pinchot.
19.0	Horseshoe Lake.
27.3	Upsidedown Creek Trailhead.

The trail: Reaching the Lake Plateau and investigating its many treasures is really a wild vacation. Don't even think about going into this area and out the next day. Instead, plan on at least two nights on the Lake Plateau, plus whatever time you take getting in and out. It is possible to get in and out with one hard day each, but most hikers take two days to reach base camp on the plateau. Bring plenty of food—after setting up camp you may decide to stay at least a week.

From the Box Canyon Trailhead, Trail 27 climbs gradually through timber and open parks along the East Fork Boulder River for about 3.5 miles before crossing a sturdy bridge. If you started late, you may wish to stay the first night at an excellent campsite just before the bridge.

Camping here is not a bad idea. Otherwise, it's a tough 11- to 14-mile day to get onto the Lake Plateau, depending on where you decide to set up base camp. And there really aren't any decent campsites at the convenient 5- to 7-mile range to split up the dis-

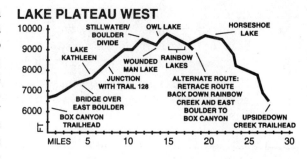

tance. So either plan to camp at the 3.5-mile mark, or aim for the valley just below the Lake Plateau, about 10 miles in, where several great campsites are nestled along Rainbow Creek.

After crossing the East Fork, the trail follows the river for 0.5 mile before climbing away through heavy timber. Several trout-filled pools beckon along the riverside stretch, so be prepared to fight off temptations to stop and rig up the fly-casting gear.

After about 2 miles Trail 27 heads south toward Slough Creek Divide. Turn left here on Trail 28.

In a couple hundred yards the trail passes little Lake Kathleen on the left. Then, 2 miles farther, Trail 128 breaks off to the right and heads for Columbine Pass. Stay left on Trail 28.

After another 3 miles, the trail meets Trail 211. At this point travelers have to decide where they intend to base camp. Here are a few options: (1) Head left up the steep switchbacks 0.75 mile to the junction with Trail 26. Bear right to any of six Rainbow Lakes to the northwest. (2) Go right less than 1 mile up Trail 211 to Fish Lake, reached after a short, steep climb. Or (3), continue past Fish Lake another 3.5 miles on Trail 211 to Lake Pinchot. All three options have plenty of great campsites.

On the way to Lake Pinchot, Wounded Man Lake might look like a good place to base camp, but it has limited campsites. Lake Pinchot adds those extra 2 or 3 miles when you really don't want them, but this beautiful lake is like the heart of the Lake Plateau. If you don't base camp here, be sure to visit on a day trip.

If you can't make up your mind on where to base camp, set up a temporary camp for one night and then spend the next day trekking around, enjoying the scenery, fishing, and searching for that five-star campsite. Then return to the temporary camp early enough to move everything to the chosen base camp site.

Once base camp is established, start taking advantage of the numerous adventures waiting in all directions. For anglers, there are two dozen lakes within the reach of an easy day hike. For climbers, there are 11,298-foot Mount Douglas, 11,153-foot Chalice Peak, and other summits to reach.

To return to the Box Canyon Trailhead, follow whichever leg of Trail 211 you didn't take on the way in. This way you will have covered the entire Lake Plateau circle (about a 6-mile loop). Drop back down to the junction with Trail 28 and retrace the route down Rainbow Creek.

To avoid backtracking on Trail 28, take Upsidedown Creek Trail 26, which heads west from the foot of Lower Rainbow Lake. Plan on two days to get out, camping at Horseshoe or Diamond lakes (sometimes called Upper and Lower Horseshoe

EXPLORING THE LAKE PLATEAU

Any trip to the Lake Plateau should include some extra time for exploring the many hidden treasures in the area. Here's a list of suggestions rated for difficulty as follows: "Human" (easy for almost everyone, including children), "Semi-Human" (moderately difficult), or "Animal" (don't try it unless you're very fit and wilderness-wise). Also refer to more detailed rating information in the chapter "Using this Guidebook."

Destination	Difficulty
Lake Pinchot	Human
Flood Creek lakes	Semi-Human
Asteroid Lake Basin	Animal
Chalice Peak	Animal
Lightning Lake	Animal
Lake Diaphanous	Human
Fish Lake	Human
Barrier Lake	Animal
Mirror Lake	Semi-Human
Chickadee Lake	Animal
Squeeze Lake	Animal
Mount Douglas	Animal
Lake Plateau Loop	Human
Martes Lake	Semi-Human
Columbine Pass	Human
Jordan Lake	Human
Sundown Lake	Semi-Human
Pentad & Favonius lakes	Human
Burnt Gulch Lake	Animal

lakes), before heading out Upsidedown Creek. This route may be slightly shorter, but it involves a steep downhill after a 600-foot climb. The trail hits the Boulder River Road about 1.5 miles north of the Box Canyon Trailhead.

It seems slightly easier to do this trip as noted above. But the route could be reversed: going in Upsidedown Creek and out along the East Fork. Be prepared for a steady, dry, 7-mile climb to Horseshoe Lake. Take extra water.

The Lake Plateau gets more use than most areas in the Beartooths, but a large number of destinations and campsites dilutes the crowd to a tolerable level. A week in this wonderland will undoubtedly be a memorable vacation. So expect a few remorseful moments when you realize that you must return to your hectic lifestyle back home. Be forewarned—the first days back at work may seem quite unpleasant.

➤ **Fishing information:** The lakes of the Lake Plateau are located in both the Stillwater and Boulder drainages and offer cutthroat, rainbow, and some golden trout fishing. Keep in mind that not all lakes contain fish; ask for specific information rather than just "trying your luck." Most of the lakes along the trails have self-sustaining populations and contain plenty of fish.

Golden trout were once planted on the plateau, but only a few remnants remain. Flood Creek, including Lake Pinchot, has beautiful mixed species of fish (golden, cutthroat, rainbow), due to migrations of planted fish. A small drainage south of Flood Creek (Asteroid Lake) contains pure goldens.

For solitude, visit one of the lakes, such as Burnt Gulch Lake or Barrier Lake, slightly off the trail. Many high mountain streams are too steep to harbor large populations of trout, so look for the slow spots.

3 COLUMBINE PASS LOOP

General description:	A five- or six-night trip and an attractive alternative to Lake Plateau West trip for those who prefer to keep moving instead of base camp.
Total distance:	34.3 miles.
Difficulty:	Moderate.
Special attractions:	A gorgeous, lake-dotted, high-altitude plateau, plus the equally spectacular Columbine Pass.
Topo maps:	USGS—Mount Douglas, Tumble Mountain, Pinnacle Mountain, and Haystack Peak; RMS—Mount Douglas-Mount Wood and Cooke City-Cutoff Mountain.

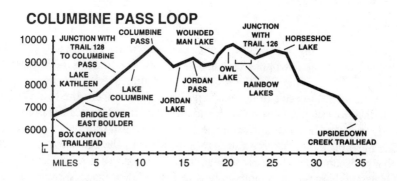

34

Lake Columbine from Columbine Pass.

Key Points:

3.5	East Fork Boulder River.
5.2	Junction with Trail 28.
5.4	Lake Kathleen.
7.9	Junction with Trail 128.
9.3	Columbine Lake.
11.1	Columbine Pass.
12.5	Pentad Lake.
14.5	Jordan Lake.
15.9	Jordan Pass.
18.7	Wounded Man Lake.
19.5	Lake Pinchot.
21.0	Rainbow Lakes.
22.5	Junction with Trail 26.
25.9	Horseshoe Lake.
34.3	Upsidedown Creek Trailhead.

The trail: The Columbine Pass Loop isn't the type of trip to choose on the spur of the moment. It's more of a vacation that should be planned months in advance, carefully mapping out a route and mindfully preparing food and equipment. Also, there aren't many opportunities like this to see so much wild country without working out a burdensome shuttle or without retracing your steps for half of the trip.

The first 8 miles are identical to the Lake Plateau West trip. It would be wise to get up early on the first day, drive to Box Canyon Trailhead, and cover at least the first 3.5 miles to the excellent campsite just before the bridge over the East Fork Boulder River. This campsite can accommodate a large party or several parties (as long as Forest Service limits for group size aren't exceeded).

After crossing the East Fork, follow the serene stream for about 0.5 mile before the trail heads into thick timber. In less than 2 miles it meets Trail 28. Trail 27 goes straight and eventually ends up in Yellowstone National Park. Turn left here on Trail 28. In about 0.25 mile, watch for tranquil little Lake Kathleen off to the left. This is also a possible first-night campsite.

About 2 miles from Lake Kathleen the trail joins Trail 128 to Columbine Pass. Turn right onto this trail, which climbs a big hill and breaks out of the forest into a subalpine panorama. From the junction it's about 1.5 miles to Lake Columbine. With an early start on the first day, this would also make a good first campsite. If it's your second day out, consider pushing on to Pentad or Jordan lakes for the second night's camp.

From Lake Columbine continue another scenic 2 miles up to 9,850-foot Columbine Pass. In a good snow year snowbanks cover the trail on Columbine Pass well into July. Also, the trail fades away twice between Lake Columbine and the pass, so watch the topo map carefully to stay on track. A few well-placed cairns make navigation here easier.

Columbine Pass is a good spot to enjoy a snack and the vistas, including 10,685-foot Pinnacle Mountain to the south. From here the trail leaves the Boulder River drainage behind and heads into the Stillwater River drainage. From now on, the trip leap frogs from one lake to another for the next 14 miles.

Those who camped at Lake Columbine can make it all the way into the Lake Plateau for the next night's campsite. Otherwise, plan to pitch a tent at Pentad or Jordan lakes. Pentad is more scenic, but Jordan offers better fishing (and suffers more from overuse). There are also several smaller lakes near Pentad—Mouse, Favonius, Sundown, and several unnamed lakes. Many great campsites can be found in the area, and they won't be as crowded as Jordan Lake probably will be. Don't rush to take the first campsite. Look around for a while and you'll find a better one. It might be wise to stop at the south end of Pentad anyway, as the trail is difficult to follow because of all the tangent trails created by backcountry horsemen to various campsites. To untangle the maze, check the topo map. The trail skirts the east shore of Pentad Lake heading north.

Jordan Lake, another 2 miles down the trail from Pentad, has limited camping with one campsite at the foot of the lake. The campsite is, however, large enough to serve a large party or several parties—although it may be too heavily impacted to be used by parties with stock animals.

Right at Jordan Lake, the trail meets Trail 23 dropping east down into the Middle Fork of Wounded Man Creek. Turn left (north) here on Trail 90, which climbs 1.5 miles to Jordan Pass and the Lake Plateau. This isn't much of a pass, but it's a great spot to take 15 minutes to marvel at the mountainous horizons in every direction.

If you camped last at Jordan or Pentad lakes, you have lots of options for the next night out. The closest site is at Wounded Man Lake, but this is a busy place. The best campsite is along the North Fork of Wounded Man Creek just southwest of the lake. But consider hiking the short mile northeast from Wounded Man Lake to Lake Pinchot to stay at the crown jewel of the Lake Plateau. The third option is to turn left on Trail 211 at the junction on the west side of Wounded Man Lake and stay at Owl Lake or one of the Rainbow Lakes that follow shortly thereafter. These offer some of the best base camps in the area because there are innumerable sights to see all within a short walk.

After a night or two on the plateau, follow Trail 211 along the west shore of Rainbow Lakes down to the junction with Trail 26 at the south end of Lower Rainbow Lake. Turn right (west) here, and spend the last night out at Diamond or Horseshoe lakes (sometimes called Upper and Lower Horseshoe lakes). Horseshoe Lake is probably better because it has more campsites and it leaves the shortest possible distance out Upsidedown Creek the last day. And that's still about 8.5 miles, plus the 1.5 miles some lucky volunteer has to walk or hitchhike up to the Box Canyon Trailhead to get the vehicle. Sorry, there are no real campsites anywhere from Horseshoe Lake to the Boulder River Road.

➤ | **Fishing information:** Anglers who want to fish the first day of the trip should camp near the East Fork Boulder River or Rainbow Creek, as most of the lakes along this route—including Lake Columbine—are barren. Burnt Gulch Lake is an exception, sporting dinner-sized cutthroat trout. Cutthroats dominate the fishery along this route until the Lake Plateau is reached. Cutthroats are fairly easy to catch and are frequently found along rocky shorelines on the downwind sides of lakes. Anglers often fish "past the fish" by casting out into the lake.

Once the Lake Plateau is reached there are a variety of fishing opportunities easily available, and Lake Pinchot would certainly make the desirable list, as would the entire Flood Creek chain of lakes.

4 SLOUGH CREEK DIVIDE

General description: A long shuttle unlike any other trail in the Beartooths with no lakes but a beautiful stream all the way.
Total distance: 39.4 miles.
Difficulty: Moderate.
Special attractions: Excessive remoteness and excellent chance to see wildlife, including bears.
Topo maps: USGS—Mount Douglas, Haystack Peak, Roundhead Butte, and Mount Hornaday; RMS—Mount Douglas-Mount Wood and Cooke City-Cutoff Mountain.

Key points:

3.5	East Fork Boulder River.
5.2	Junction with Trail 28.
8.2	Junction with unnumbered trail to Wool Lake.
9.5	Junction with Trail 104 to Independence Peak.
10.0	Slough Creek Divide.
11.8	Slough Creek.
15.7	Junction with Trail 309 up Wounded Man Creek.
17.0	Junction with Trail 9 to Horseshoe Basin.
21.1	Junction with Trail 84 up Lake Abundance Creek.
22.2	Junction with Trail 84 up Bull Creek.
24.9	Junction with Trail 193 up Wolverine Creek.
25.2	Slough Creek Guard Station.
26.2	Junction with Trail 102 up Tucker Creek.
28.0	Silver Tip Ranch.
28.4	Yellowstone National Park boundary.
31.4	Junction with trail up to Bliss Pass.
39.4	Slough Creek Campground.

The trail: Most of the Beartooths is subalpine: open, rocky country full of mountainous panoramas. But not this trail. Instead, this trail starts in the deep forest of the upper Boulder River Valley and stays below timberline for about 40 miles.

This is one of the most phenomenal trails in the Beartooths. Yet during the summer it doesn't get much use, mainly because the trail doesn't go to a lake or the top of a mountain and it requires a very time-consuming shuttle. In the fall, however, many hunters and outfitters use the area in search of the elk, deer, and other big game common in Boulder River/Slough Creek country. If you're looking for solitude and remoteness and the chance to see all kinds of wildlife, put this trail high on your list of priorities.

The first step is to arrange a shuttle. This route can be done from either end, but starting at the north end is slightly better because it allows a net loss in elevation and the trip ends up in Yellowstone National Park. If your group is big enough to split in two, start at opposite ends and trade keys when you meet each other. This greatly reduces the trouble in arranging the shuttle. If not, leave a vehicle at the Slough Creek Campground and Trailhead in Yellowstone National Park and drive all the way around (about a four-hour drive) to the Box Canyon Trailhead at the end of

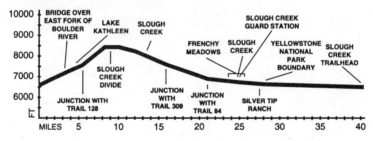

SLOUGH CREEK DIVIDE

the Boulder River Road.

The second step is to call the backcountry office at Yellowstone National Park (307-344-7381) and ask about camping in Slough Creek. The park has a policy of not giving out backcountry camping permits more than 48 hours in advance. If you plan to camp in Slough Creek in the park on the way out, you'll need one of these permits. You'll also need an exception to the 48-hour policy. Be sure to contact the park far enough in advance to get the permit before you leave. Otherwise, you won't be able to camp in the park without a permit and you'll have at least 11 miles to cover on the last day of the trip. If you plan carefully, you might be able to pick up the permit and arrange shuttle transportation at the same time.

It's best to do the shuttle early in the day and start in the afternoon so you can spend the first night at the East Fork Boulder River. Either stay where the trail first crosses the river about 3.5 miles up the trail or at the second crossing 2 miles later just after the junction with Trail 28, which goes north into the Lake Plateau. At this junction, go straight, staying on Trail 27. In about 0.25 mile the trail turns south and crosses the East Fork. There's also a good campsite here, but no bridge.

After crossing the East Fork a second time, the trail narrows down to the normal size from the broad "two-lane." It then heads gradually uphill for about 5 miles to the Slough Creek Divide.

The Slough Creek Divide is a wonderful place. It's well signed and is, surprisingly, the highest point of the trip: a mere 8,576 feet, significantly below timberline and unusually low for the Beartooths.

On the way up here, be wary not to accidentally get on the side trail heading up to Wool Lake (not named on USGS topo map). When the trail meets the stream coming down from Lamb (not named on USGS topo map) and Blue lakes, it's all too easy to follow the trail up the right side of the stream. Instead, stay on Trail 27, which crosses the stream at that point.

A excellent choice for a second campsite would be the huge open park at the headwaters of the East Fork about 0.25 mile before the divide. This differs from most campsites in the Beartooths, but it's no disappointment. Campers can spend lots of time marveling at the view across the lush meadow at Monument Peak and Haystack Peak. About halfway through the big meadow the trail comes to a junction with Trail 104 to the ghost town of Independence. This trail leads back to the end of the jeep road that continues on past the Box Canyon Trailhead. Bear left here, crossing the East Fork for the third and last time, and go straight (southeast) on Trail 104.

The next 10 miles are not good trail for people deathly afraid of bears. Tracks, scat, and other sign of the Great Bear are usually evident along the trail, as this area supports a healthy grizzly population.

Another great campsite is found about 2 miles from the last crossing of the East Fork when the trail first hits Slough Creek. Keep in mind that this is bear country, so be extra careful with food and garbage, including fish entrails.

From this point on, the trail follows Slough Creek all the way to Yellowstone Park. After dropping off the divide, there's an unmarked trail junction with a fairly good trail going off to the right (southwest). Bear left (southeast) here; going right ends up on the west side of the stream on a trail that the Forest Service is in the process of abandoning. Some maps also show parallel trails going down both sides of Slough

Creek; stay on the east side of the creek.

Good campsites are common in the frequent meadows at least until the junction with Trail 309 that goes up Wounded Man Creek. Incidentally, this is not any relation to the Wounded Man Creek leaving the Lake Plateau and rushing down into the Stillwater River, the next major drainage east of Slough Creek. It would be interesting to know why we have two streams with the same name in the same area, but nobody seems to know. The dramatic fires of 1988 scorched the Slough Creek drainage all the way up to Wounded Man Creek.

The side trails up Wounded Man Creek, Horseshoe Basin, and Lake Abundance are not regularly maintained. Explorers who want to take a side trip up any of these drainages should allow plenty of time for finding the trail and climbing over deadfall from the 1988 burn. Expect to find quiet and utter solitude. The Forest Service attempts to clear these trails once every four years, but they are still in poor shape.

For the third night out, push on to excellent campsites at Lake Abundance Creek and Bull Creek. Or camp anywhere along upper Slough Creek. Those looking for solitude might want to avoid camping right at Bull Creek, the site of a large outfitter camp.

Just after Bull Creek, the trail breaks out into oversized Frenchy Meadow, a privately owned inholding that has been cultivated in the past, witnessed by some old farm equipment rusting away here and there. At the south end of the meadow stands the Slough Creek Guard Station and accompanying corrals, managed by the Forest Service.

About 3 miles farther the trail arrives at the Silver Tip Ranch, a private inholding within the Absaroka-Beartooth Wilderness and precisely on the northern boundary of Yellowstone Park. Remember that this is private land, so hurry through. There's a gate at each end; be sure to leave the gate the way you found it. Rest assured, however, that you aren't trespassing. The Forest Service has a conservation easement that allows the public to cross both Frenchy Meadows and the Silver Tip Ranch. Sometime in the future the Forest Service plans to re-route the trail around the Silver Tip Ranch.

The park boundary is right after the south end of the ranch. The trail from the park boundary to the trailhead is actually a two-lane road, and it would be physically possible to drive all the way up Slough Creek to the Silver Tip Ranch from the Slough Creek Campground in the park. This, however, is strictly prohibited. The only vehicle allowed on this trail is a horse-drawn wagon operated by the owners of the Silver Tip Ranch.

A good choice for the fourth night out would be one of the three designated campsites in Yellowstone Park—if you have a permit. If you don't have a campsite reserved, then arrange your earlier campsites so you can camp somewhere between the Slough Creek Guard Station and the Silver Tip Ranch. Unfortunately, this leaves 11 miles or more out on the last day. This won't be that bad, as the last leg of the trip is an easy, stream-grade, downhill walk along lower Slough Creek.

Slough Creek is world famous for its large cutthroat trout. Expect to see anglers fly casting the slow waters of Slough Creek as it meanders through an expansive meadow. In fact, the entire lower Slough Creek Valley is bordered by lush meadows.

➤ **Fishing information:** Of all the 944 lakes in the Beartooths, a few lakes in the Slough Creek Drainage may have been the only ones that originally contained fish. Both Heather and Peace lakes, for example, contain indigenous Yellowstone cutthroat trout. There is no record of fish being planted in either lake, although there have been plants of Yellowstone cutthroats in Slough Creek.

This trail offers anglers a choice of cutthroat trout or cutthroat trout, with a possibility of an errant rainbow from the East Fork Boulder River side of the divide. Blue Lake is the only lake near the route, on the Boulder side, with fish—nice fat cutthroat trout.

Slough Creek is the premier cutthroat trout stream fishery in Montana, although a great deal of it is found in Yellowstone Park. Anglers need a special fishing permit from Yellowstone National Park to fish Slough Creek in the park. Current park regulations call for catch-and-release fishing. Be sure to check both Montana and Yellowstone regulations before wetting a line.

TRAILHEAD 2
WEST STILLWATER

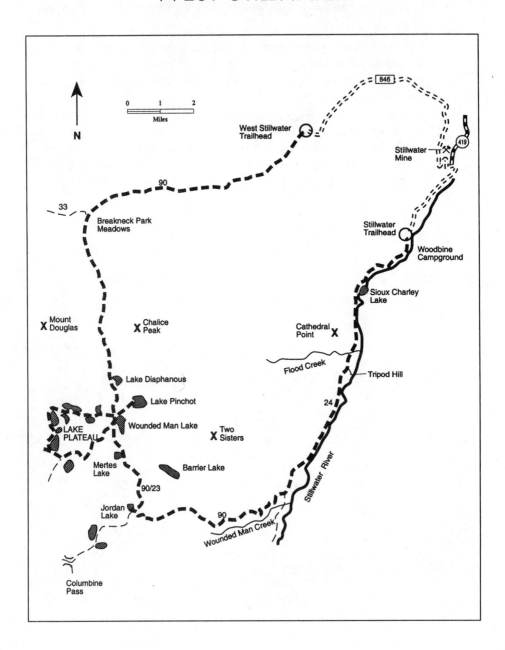

West Stillwater Trailhead

846

Stillwater Mine

419

Stillwater Trailhead

Woodbine Campground

90

33

Breakneck Park Meadows

Sioux Charley Lake

X Mount Douglas

X Chalice Peak

Cathedral Point X

Flood Creek

Tripod Hill

Lake Diaphanous

Lake Pinchot

Wounded Man Lake

X Two Sisters

24

LAKE PLATEAU

Mertes Lake

Barrier Lake

Stillwater River

90/23

Jordan Lake

90

Wounded Man Creek

Columbine Pass

0   1   2
Miles

N

OVERVIEW

The West Stillwater Trailhead receives much less use than trailheads to the east (Stillwater River) or to the west (Boulder River), but not due to a shortage of scenic attributes or excellent trails. To the contrary, the trail up the West Stillwater is definitely worth seeing.

Perhaps one reason for the lower use is tougher access. Unlike the Boulder and Stillwater (and most other major river drainages in Montana), the West Stillwater does not have an access road along its shores. Instead, travelers have to take a rough Forest Service gravel road over the ridge separating the West Stillwater and the Stillwater drainages to get to the West Stillwater Trailhead.

One interesting peculiarity of this trailhead is that the wilderness boundary has been extended downstream to the trailhead to include more of the river and its critical riparian habitat, mainly to protect this critical area from future mining development.

FINDING THE TRAILHEAD

From Interstate 90 at Columbus drive 15 miles south on Montana Highway 78 to Absarokee. Continue south from town about 2 miles and turn right on the Nye Road (County Road 419). Drive about 25 miles southwest, through Nye, to the Stillwater Mine (which is about 2 miles before the Stillwater Trailhead and Woodbine Campground at road's end). Immediately after the mine, turn right (west) on Forest Road 846 at a well-marked intersection. From here it's a long 8 miles to the trailhead.

There's a vehicle campground about 1 mile before the trailhead. Although the parking area is smaller than the Boulder or Stillwater trailheads, there's still plenty of room to park. Large horse trailers might have some difficulty.

THE TRAILS

> Breakneck Park Meadows
> Lake Plateau North
> Stillwater to Stillwater

5 BREAKNECK PARK MEADOWS

General description: An excellent overnight trip or long day trip.
Total distance: 16 miles.
Difficulty: Moderate.
Special attractions: An unusually large, gorgeous mountain meadow.
Topo maps: USGS—Picket Pin Mountain and Tumble Mountain; RMS—Mount Douglas-Mount Wood.

Key points:
3.4 Crescent Creek.
7.8 Divide Creek.
8.0 Breakneck Park Meadows.

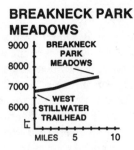

The trail: Those who want to see a remote and beautiful mountain river drainage without making it a week-long trip should try an overnighter into Breakneck Park Meadows. The hike in and out can be done in a day, but it's a long haul—about 16 miles.

The well-maintained trail closely follows the West Stillwater most of the way, hugging the north and west bank. But just before Breakneck Park Meadows it gradually climbs out of sight of the stream through several smaller meadows. Some of these clearings seem big enough to be a worthy destination, but there's no mistaking the expanse of Breakneck Park Meadows when you get there. The trail hits Breakneck Park Meadows about 0.25 mile above the West Stillwater. Take a break here and look around for that ideal campsite. Campers who want a fire can usually find enough wood nearby.

Most visitors just want to relax, fish, or watch for deer, moose, or elk, all abundant in the area. But for an interesting side trip, take the trail leaving Breakneck Park Meadows about halfway through and climb the 3 miles to Breakneck Plateau at the foot of 10,232-foot Breakneck Mountain.

Even though it's an 8-mile return trip to the trailhead, this stretch goes fast because of the gradual gradient and the excellent condition of the trail.

➤ | **Fishing information:** The West Fork of the Stillwater River harbors a mixed fishing opportunity. The lower reaches have brown trout, brook trout, and rainbow trout. The browns phase out upstream leaving rainbows and brookies, while cutthroats start to appear. The upper West Fork contains mostly cutthroats.

6 *LAKE PLATEAU NORTH*

General description: A long, base-camp trip into the Lake Plateau.
Total distance: 34 miles.
Difficulty: Moderate, but long.
Special attractions: A beautiful and natural mountain stream, the West Stillwater River, follows much of the trail.
Topo maps: USGS—Pickett Pin Mountain and Tumble Mountain; RMS—Mount Douglas-Mount Wood.

Key points:

- 8.0   Breakneck Park Meadows.
- 9.5   First bridge over the West Stillwater.
- 14.3   Lewis Creek Bridge over the West Stillwater.
- 16.2   Lake Diaphanous.
- 17.0   Wounded Man Lake.

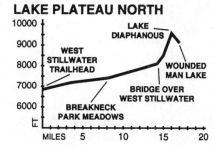

LAKE PLATEAU NORTH

The trail: The West Stillwater provides the third major access route, along with the East Fork Boulder and Stillwater rivers, into this popular, high plateau. It also provides the longest and most remote route, but it may be the easiest because of the absence of any steep climbs.

Even though this trail might not be as popular as others in the Beartooths, it's still in wonderful condition, well-maintained and easy to follow. It follows the West Stillwater for 17 miles to Lake Diaphanous, crossing two major bridges along the way. So don't worry about getting wet feet.

Most travelers will probably want to take two days to reach a base camp on the Lake Plateau. Fortunately, the West Stillwater accommodates this schedule with a perfect campsite at the halfway point, Breakneck Park Meadows. Although the trail into Breakneck Park Meadows is interrupted by several beautiful smaller meadows, the expansive Breakneck Park Meadows is exceptional and much larger. Campers can choose from many grand tent sites with plenty of wood for a campfire.

After leaving Breakneck Park Meadows the trail worsens slightly but is still excellent. The stream gradient increases slightly, but there are no big climbs. The trail bridges the West Stillwater and then hits its steepest grade for about 1 mile. Even this is much less of a climb than coming into the plateau from the east or west.

The trail continues along the east bank for just under 2 miles to the Lewis Creek Bridge, which crosses not Lewis Creek but a small branch of the West Stillwater. From here the trail climbs another 2 miles to the plateau and Lake Diaphanous. This small, high-altitude lake has one excellent campsite. Lake Diaphanous lies above timberline, and the views are fantastic. Even though there are a few trees around the campsite, the wood supply is too scant for a campfire.

Most people prefer to go into the Lake Plateau for a base camp. Wounded Man Lake is just another 0.8 mile down the trail, and there are many excellent campsites at neighboring lakes to choose from. Take some extra time to find that five-star campsite.

The side trip to lovely Lightning Lake is enticing, but it isn't easy. There are two route options. Scramble up Lightning Creek, which joins the West Stillwater about 5 miles from the trailhead. Or leap frog over Chalice Peak from Lake Diaphanous. Be wary of the trip up Lightning Creek. It's shorter, but it's very steep and difficult. Although the cross-country trip over Chalice Peak looks long and difficult, it really isn't that difficult. If you try it, you may experience one of your best days ever in the wilderness—if you are in good shape, leave camp at or before daybreak, and the weather is good.

After spending a few enjoyable days on the Lake Plateau, return down the West Stillwater, an equally enjoyable, gradual downhill all the way.

> **Fishing information:** This trail follows the West Fork of the Stillwater (see the stream fishery description in the Breakneck Park Meadows section). Lake Diaphanous is in the main Stillwater drainage and supports some nice rainbows. Expect company, as this is a logical place to stop coming and going. From here, it's straight downhill, southeast to Lake Pinchot for great camping, and fishing for beautiful hybrids of golden, cutthroat, and rainbow descent. Flood Creek itself provides a pretty good alpine fishery and would be worth a try. There are pure golden trout in Asteroid and some of the surrounding lakes, but getting there isn't easy.
>
> The Lake Plateau offers a variety of fishing opportunities, mostly for rainbow and cutthroat trout, and most of the lakes along trails harbor fish. For solitude, get off the trails, but ask beforehand to learn which lakes hold fish before counting on trout for dinner.

7 STILLWATER TO STILLWATER

General description: A long shuttle through the Lake Plateau.
Total distance: 38.5 miles.
Difficulty: Moderate, but long.
Special attractions: A rare chance to follow two splendid mountain rivers through the wilderness and, along the way, see the famous Lake Plateau.
Topo maps: USGS—Cathedral Point, Little Park Mountain, Pinnacle Mountain, Tumble Mountain, and Pickett Pin Mountain; RMS—Mount Douglas-Mount Wood and Cooke City-Cutoff Mountain.

Key points:
8.0	Breakneck Park Meadows.
9.5	First bridge over West Stillwater.
14.3	Lewis Creek Bridge over West Stillwater.
16.2	Lake Diaphanous.
17.0	Wounded Man Lake.
20.3	Jordan Pass.
21.5	Jordan Lake.
28.5	Junction with Stillwater Trail 24.
32.3	Tripod Hill.
33.0	Flood Creek.
35.5	Sioux Charley Lake.
38.5	Stillwater River Trailhead.

The trail: If you can arrange a shuttle and want to see lots of wild country in one week, there's no use making the West Stillwater a base-camp trip. Instead, just keep going through the Lake Plateau and out to civilization at the Stillwater River Trailhead

STILLWATER TO STILLWATER

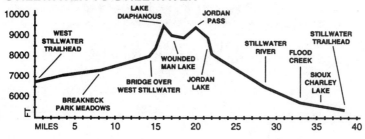

and Woodbine Campground.

For the first part of the trail, refer to the West Stillwater Trail. But instead of setting up a base camp at Lake Diaphanous, Wounded Man Lake, or one of the numerous campsites on the Lake Plateau, stay there only one or two nights. Then head south from Wounded Man Lake on Trail 90 over Jordan Pass to Jordan Lake. Consider staying at Jordan Lake before heading down Wounded Man Creek, still on Trail 90. Jordan Lake gets lots of use, so even though it's a forested lake, camp softly and skip the campfire that night.

A good choice for the last night out would be the confluence of Wounded Man Creek and the Stillwater River or at a huge open area along the river about 1 mile farther down the trail.

Be sure to read through the West Stillwater and Lake Plateau East trail descriptions before hitting the trail.

➤ | **Fishing information:** Note the fisheries information from the Breakneck Park Meadows portion for fish on the West Fork.

This circular route offers fewer opportunities to sample the lakes of the Lake Plateau, but there's still plenty of good fishing along the way. There are rainbows in Lake Diaphanous, rainbows and cutthroats in Wounded Man Lake, and the interesting fishery noted earlier in the Flood Creek drainage.

The Wounded Man Creek drainage supports a mainly cutthroat trout fishery, although rainbows are present with cutthroats in Pentad and Favonius lakes, up the middle fork. Jordan Lake holds nice cutthroats, which can be counted on to provide dinner.

Lakes off the trail also offer good fishing, with Martes providing a nice cutthroat fishery, three to five years after each plant. Aufwuchs Lake requires a tough hike to reach secluded cutthroats, but it might be worth the effort.

Heading out along the main Stillwater River can provide a lot of pan-sized trout for hungry hikers. There is a mixture of cutthroats, rainbows, and brookies to be had with minimal effort. Much of the slower water is dominated by brookies; please eat them—they taste great!

TRAILHEAD 3
STILLWATER RIVER

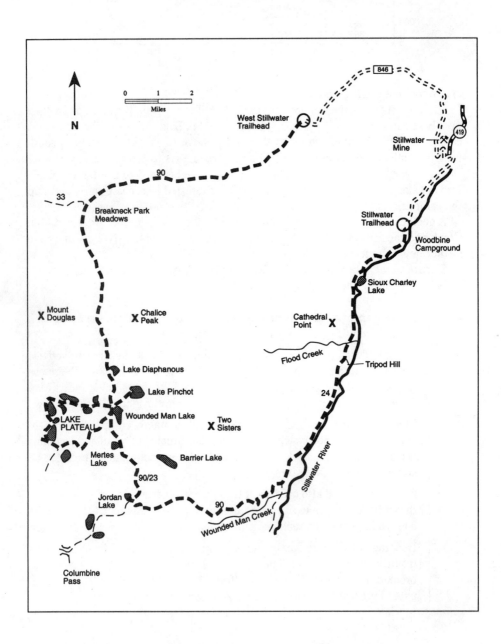

The Stillwater River actually has some still water. Michael S. Sample photo.

OVERVIEW

The Stillwater River Trailhead is one of the most accessible and heavily used access points to the Beartooths. It's also a large trailhead with toilet facilities and plenty of parking and a large Forest Service campground, Woodbine.

Getting there is a treat. The drive up the Stillwater River is one of the most scenic in Montana. The Stillwater River flows majestically through a landscape dominated by large ranches interspersed with small ranching communities like Fishtail, Nye, Beehive, Dean, and Moraine. Watch for bighorn sheep near the Stillwater Mine.

The Stillwater River carries more water out of the Beartooths than any other stream, and it's certainly one of the most beautiful drainages. Nowadays, however, it is a little less wild than in the recent past. The north rim of the Beartooths, and especially the Stillwater River area, is highly mineralized. In recent years, several controversial mining developments have sprung up in this area, including some very large operations. The rapid growth of mines and the associated residential development has brought many more people into this remote part of Montana.

FINDING THE TRAILHEAD

This is one of the easiest trailheads to find. In fact, you can't miss it. From Interstate 90 at Columbus, drive 15 miles south on Montana Highway 78 to Absarokee. Continue south 2 miles and turn west on the paved Nye Road (County Road 419), and go through Fishtail and Nye. Stay on this road, which eventually ends at the trailhead, about 2 miles past the Stillwater Mine. It's about 42 miles southwest of Columbus.

CROSS-REFERENCE

Be sure to check "The Complete Stillwater" trip, which starts at the Lake Abundance Trailhead and ends at the Stillwater Trailhead, and also the "Stillwater to Stillwater" trip, which starts at the West Stillwater Trailhead and ends at the Stillwater Trailhead. Both trips could be taken in reverse by starting at the Stillwater Trailhead.

THE TRAILS

Sioux Charley Lake
Lake Plateau East
Lake Wilderness

8 *SIOUX CHARLEY LAKE*

General description: A short, easy day hike.
Total distance: 6 miles.
Difficulty: Easy.
Topo maps: USGS—Cathedral Point; RMS—Mount Douglas-Mount Wood.

Key points:

0.5 Enter narrow canyon.
3.0 Sioux Charley Lake.

SIOUX CHARLEY LAKE

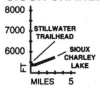

The trail: This easy day trip into Sioux Charley Lake is one of the most popular day hikes in the Beartooths, so don't be surprised to see lots of people on the trail. From the trailhead, it's 3 miles to the lake, all on an easy, consistently uphill grade.

Soon after leaving the trailhead, the trail enters a narrow canyon where, right next to the trail, the river tumbles over a series of cascades and rapids. Many a hiker has paused here to wonder why this stream was ever named the "still water."

After passing through the narrow canyon the trail winds its way through a heavy forest all the way to Sioux Charley Lake. Now the reason behind the river's name becomes clear. The lake is really just a large, slow-moving or "still" section of the river. Farther upstream, the river slows into several similar still-water stretches.

Look across the lake to the east to see the northernmost reaches of the dramatic forest fires of 1988. The Storm Creek Fire burned all the way down the Stillwater River drainage to Sioux Charley Lake, almost completely through the Beartooths.

Although this is most often considered a day trip, camping at Sioux Charley Lake is possible. The lake is very heavily used, however, so be extra careful to leave no trace while camping here. The area is already showing some wear and tear, and all of us must do our part to help it reclaim its natural character.

➤ | **Fishing information:** The Stillwater River can yield a lot of pan-sized trout. There is a mixture of rainbows and brookies, with an occasional cutthroat to be found along this route. Much of the slower water is dominated by brookies. Since brook trout tend to overpopulate (to the detriment of other species), please eat them and help out the cutts and rainbows. Catch and release doesn't improve the brookies' size—it only limits the amount of food per fish. Besides, they taste great!

Sioux Charley Lake is one of the best places to catch these tasty morsels, and the omnipresent brookies can provide dinner for many large parties.

9 *LAKE PLATEAU EAST*

General description: A long, base camp trip into Lake Plateau.
Total distance: 45 miles.
Difficulty: Moderate, but long.
Special attractions: The least used access route to Lake Plateau.
Topo maps: USGS—Cathedral Point, Little Park Mountain, Pinnacle Mountain, and Tumble Mountain; RMS—Mount Douglas-Mount Wood and Cooke City-Cutoff Mountain.

Key points:

3.0	Sioux Charley Lake.
5.5	Flood Creek.
6.2	Tripod Point.
11.0	Junction with West Stillwater Trail 90.
11.2	Wounded Man Creek.
18.0	Jordan Lake.
19.2	Jordan Pass.
22.5	Wounded Man Lake.

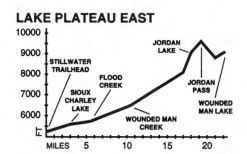

The trail: The first 11 miles of the trail follow the Stillwater River, a magnificent mountain stream, well-named for its frequent "still" sections. With the exception of the first 3 miles into Sioux Charley Lake, the Stillwater was badly burned by the 1988 fires. But the forest is rapidly coming back, and the valley is lush and moist all the way. Keep an eye open for the abundant whitetails and moose, both common along the river.

From Sioux Charley Lake the trail runs south 2.5 miles to the base of well-named Cathedral Point and a bridge over Flood Creek. Just after the bridge a side trail heads off to the left (east) up to a scenic point, aptly named Tripod Point. The overlook affords a full perspective of the grandeur of the Stillwater River drainage, and it's definitely worth the extra stroll.

Camping is available anywhere along the Stillwater River. With an early start, travelers might make it to a great campsite on a smooth stretch of river about 1 mile before the junction with Trail 90 (and about 10 miles from the trailhead). This is a slightly better campsite than camping at Wounded Man Creek. Looking at the map, some people may want to head for Roosevelt Lake as a potential campsite. But this is really Roosevelt "marsh," and it doesn't have any good campsites. Wood is abundant throughout the Stillwater for evening campfires.

Those who make good mileage on the first day can make it to Jordan Lake for the second night out. Some backpackers might choose to spend two nights along the Stillwater before climbing the 7 miles up to Jordan Lake. Bear right onto Trail 90 going up Wounded Man Creek. It's a moderately steep climb for the first 6 miles, and the last mile is a lung-buster as the trail switchbacks 700 feet up to lake.

Really ambitious hikers can take a side trip up to Barrier Lake. Where the trail crosses the North Fork of Wounded Man Creek, scramble up the stream for about 1.25 miles. After about 0.25 mile the stream disappears, but keep going. This is a very unusual lake. It looks like a reservoir that has been drawn down and has a flat bench around it. Even though the map shows a fairly large stream (the North Fork of Wounded Man Creek) leaving Barrier Lake, the lake actually has no outlet. Instead, the stream flows underground for about a mile before suddenly bursting out of the rocks as a giant spring and the North Fork of Wounded Man Creek is reborn. Notice that the North Fork has very cold water, almost painful to drink.

Jordan Lake is a delightful place with several campsites on the south end just east of where the trail hits the lake. Together, the sites make a camping area large enough to accommodate a large party or two or three small parties. The campsite is marginal for campfires, but if a fire is absolutely needed there is an adequate supply of firewood in the area.

For a great side trip from Jordan Lake, get up early the next morning and take Trail 97 from the south end of the lake over to Columbine Pass. Along the way the trail skirts Pentad and Favonius lakes, and the scenery is magnificent, especially near the pass.

To continue the main hike from Jordan Lake, head north, still on Trail 90, for almost 5 miles over Jordan Pass to Wounded Man Lake. Jordan Pass is a very easy climb from Jordan Lake, so don't fret over it. Actually, there's another climb just before Wounded Man Lake that's much more difficult.

Once at Wounded Man Lake, spend some time selecting a good site for base camp. There are many options such as the Rainbow Lakes to the west or Lake Pinchot to the east. The best campsite at Wounded Man Lake is just southwest of the lake. Wherever you land, spend at least two more days enjoying and exploring the Lake Plateau before retracing your steps back down the Stillwater to the trailhead.

➤ | **Fishing information:** This trail offers less opportunity to sample lakes on the way to the Lake Plateau, but there's plenty of good fishing along the way. Heading up along the main Stillwater River can provide a lot of great fishing for lunch-sized trout. There is a mixture of cutthroats, rainbows, and brookies to be had without much effort. Much of the slower water is dominated by brookies, with cutthroats becoming more common as you get closer to Wounded Man Creek.

Wounded Man Creek supports a mainly cutthroat trout fishery, although rainbows share Pentad and Favionus lakes with cutts. Jordan Lake holds nice cutthroats that can be counted on to provide dinner.

Lakes off the trail also provide good fishing, with Martes providing a nice cutthroat fishery three to five years after each plant. Martes is on an eight-year cycle; 1995 was the last year fish were planted. Aufwuchs Lake is a tough cross-country hike to secluded cutthroats, but it might be worth the effort.

Beautiful hybrids live in Lake Pinchot and along Flood Creek. The Lake Plateau offers a variety of fishing opportunities, consisting mostly of rainbow and cutthroat trout.

10 *LAKE WILDERNESS*

General description: A little-used, off-trail overnighter.
Total distance: 14 miles.
Difficulty: Mostly off-trail and difficult.
Special attractions: Extraordinary mountain scenery and solitude, and a favorite of climbers.
Topo maps: USGS—Mount Wood; RMS—Mount Douglas-Mount Wood.

Key points:

2.0 Snow chute; end of established trail.
6.0 Edge of plateau, drop down to Lake Wilderness.

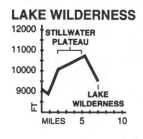

LAKE WILDERNESS

The trail: To do this mostly off-trail, high-elevation trip, hikers must be proficient with compass and topo map—and be well-conditioned. Also wait for good weather, but prepare for the worst in case a storm blows in.

The unofficial Lake Wilderness trailhead is difficult to find, so allow for some extra time to get there. Turn southwest off County Road 419 between Dean and Nye on the Benbow Mine Road. Follow the road 12 miles to the mine. Go by the mine and after 0.5 mile or so, the road turns west and switchbacks another 0.5 mile up to "The Golf Course," a large, open meadow that long ago somebody thought looked like a golf course. The poorly marked trailhead is at the south end of The Golf Course, right by a lone fence post where the road gradually narrows to become a trail. Most passenger cars can traverse the road up to the mine, but after the mine, a high-clearance vehicle is essential.

The well-defined trail heads off in a southerly direction from The Golf Course above Benbow Mine. It immediately (but briefly) descends into a forested saddle and then climbs gradually up to the magnificent Stillwater Plateau. After a few short zigzags, the trail heads off to the west. The second mile of the trail is lined with cairns

LAKE WILDERNESS

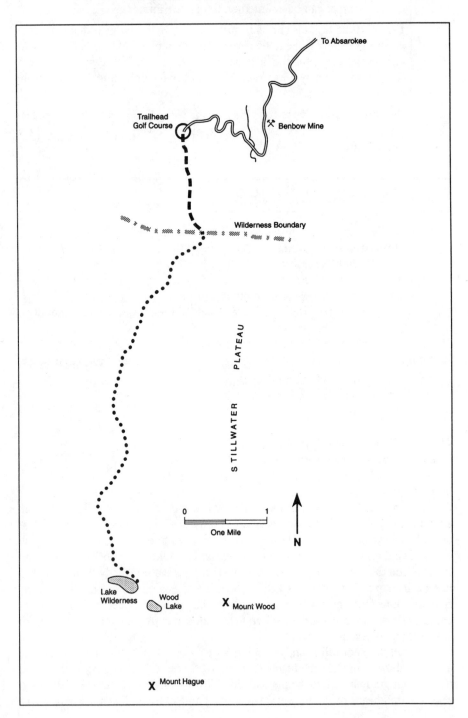

To Absarokee

Trailhead
Golf Course

Benbow Mine

Wilderness Boundary

PLATEAU

STILLWATER

0   1
One Mile

N

Lake
Wilderness

Wood
Lake

X Mount Wood

X Mount Hague

even though the tread is distinct.

After 2 miles, at 10,000 feet and at the head of a snow chute, the trail disappears. Get out the topo map and compass and keep them handy for the next 4 miles until Lake Wilderness is in sight.

Take off cross-country bearing southwest for about a mile and then turn south for about another 2.5 miles. Be sure to continue climbing gradually, trying to stay on or slightly above the 10,500-foot contour instead of dropping elevation to where cliffs block the way. As soon as you get close to the steepening slopes of 12,661-foot Mount Wood, look off to the south to see Lake Wilderness.

There's no graceful way to get down the 1,000-foot drop to the lake, but it's slightly better to head out across the talus slope to the left into the forest until you intersect the inlet stream and then follow the stream to the lake.

Campsites are limited at Lake Wilderness, but look for spots for small parties along the north shore and near the outlet. There's also a possible campsite in a meadow about 0.25 mile northwest of the lake. The outlet stream is deep and difficult to ford. Wood is plentiful, so enjoy a campfire.

For a great side trip, take the 0.5-mile scramble over to Wood Lake. It's a short but tough trip. Wood Lake has deep emerald green water and a fantastic backdrop of Mount Wood and 12,328-foot Mount Hague. A fluted, cathedral-like wall extends across the saddle between the two peaks creating a gothic effect.

Camping is even more limited at Wood Lake than Lake Wilderness, so it's better to visit this lovely spot on a side trip and camp elsewhere.

➤ | **Fishing information:** Lake Wilderness supports a nice population of cutthroat trout. Wood Lake is stocked with cutthroats, by helicopter, on an eight-year cycle (due again in 1997). Fly fishing in both lakes is tough because of the forested shoreline. Any fish in nearby streams will be migrants from these lakes.

TRAILHEAD 4
WEST ROSEBUD

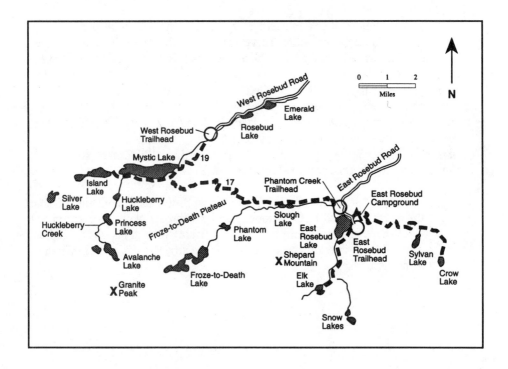

OVERVIEW

The West Rosebud Trailhead is one of the most unusual in the Beartooths. The trail starts in a Montana Power Company work area, and for the first 2 miles or so it climbs to a manmade dam on Mystic Lake. The dam raised the water level of the natural lake, making Mystic the deepest lake in the Beartooths (more than 200 feet). Plus, two delightful lakes—Emerald and West Rosebud—lie right at the trailhead.

Located about 80 miles southwest of Billings, the West Rosebud is similar to the East Rosebud and other trailheads on the northern face of the Beartooths. The gravel access road follows a beautiful stream (West Rosebud Creek) through traditional Montana ranching country, mostly undeveloped. The road may be rough in sections, but it can be negotiated easily by any two-wheel-drive vehicle. Besides, the scenery is well worth the bumps. Travelers can see the narrow valley opening up in the mountains long before they arrive.

This area also resembles East Rosebud because of the little community at the trailhead. Instead of summer cabins, however, the structures at this trailhead house workers employed by the owner of Mystic Dam Power Station, the Montana Power Company.

The West Rosebud is the only major drainage in the Beartooths that's closed to horse traffic during the summer. This is due to hazardous rock fields and snow drifts common on a section of trail just before Mystic Lake early in the season. Horses are allowed into the area, however, during the fall big-game hunting seasons, usually starting in mid-September.

A short way up the trail, look for a plaque placed in a stone in memory of Mark E. Von Seggern, a Boy Scout from Columbus who died in 1979 after a tragic slide down a snowbank near Mystic Lake.

The plaque also offers that age-old (but never out-of-date) advice—"Be Prepared." This is especially true for weekend adventurers heading up to Froze-to-Death Plateau to climb Montana's highest mountain, Granite Peak. Actually, Granite isn't a difficult climb for experienced climbers, but many people going up the mountain aren't that experienced. Perhaps the plaque will remind them that at least they should be prepared.

FINDING THE TRAILHEAD

To find the West Rosebud Trailhead, drive 15 miles south from Columbus on Montana Highway 78 to Absarokee. Continue through Absarokee about 2 miles and turn right (west) to Fishtail. Drive through Fishtail and go west and south about 1 mile. Turn left (south) along the West Rosebud Road. About 6 miles later, take another left (southeast) at the sign for West Rosebud Lake. It's another 14 miles of bumpy gravel road from this point to the trailhead. In total, it's 27 miles from Absarokee and 42 miles from Columbus. The road ends and the trail begins right at the Mystic Dam Power Station.

There is a spacious parking lot and toilet facilities at the trailhead. But it might not seem clear exactly where the trail begins. After parking your vehicle, walk up the road about 200 yards through the Montana Power Company compound to the actual trailhead.

11 *MYSTIC LAKE*

General description:	An easy day trip.
Total distance:	7 miles.
Difficulty:	Moderate.
Special attractions:	Mystic Lake, definitely worth the trip, and the Mystic Lake hydroelectric project.
Topo maps:	USGS—Granite Peak and Alpine; RMS—Cooke City-Cutoff Mountain.

The trail: For those who aren't interested in strenuous mountain climbing or long arduous trips, the Mystic Lake trail offers an excellent choice for an unhurried day in the wilderness. It also offers some spectacular scenery with the unusual twist of being able to observe how the Mystic Lake Power Station was built.

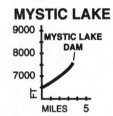

Besides being a popular day trip, this is also the major launching point for the legions who attempt to climb Granite Peak each year. Don't expect to have the trail all to yourself.

After crossing an overpass and a bridge over West Rosebud Creek, the trail follows a power line for a short way. After leaving this "sign of civilization" behind, the trail switchbacks through open rock fields, offering a great view of the West Rosebud Valley, including West Rosebud and Emerald lakes below.

The climb doesn't seem that steep, but by the time the trail reaches the dam, it has ascended 1,200 feet in 3 miles. Normally, that would be considered a big climb, but for hikers who aren't in a hurry, it really doesn't seem like it.

When the trail finally breaks out over the ridge, it affords a great view of Mystic Dam. Mystic Lake is a natural lake, but the dam increased its size and depth. The sandy beach along the east shore of the lake below is perhaps the largest in the Beartooths.

This makes a good lunch spot for those who plan to turn back for the trailhead. But it's far better to set aside enough time to walk along the lake for a while. The trail is very scenic, flat, and well maintained. Plus, it's difficult to realize the full scope of Mystic Lake from the first overlook. This is a huge lake, and a walk along its shore is the best way to appreciate this fact.

Several camp spots are found along Mystic's east shore, but the shoreline seems more suited to leisurely day hiking.

Some people might think that the presence of the dam detracts from the wildness of the place. But Montana Power Company has done as much as possible to keep the intrusion to a minimum, and after all, the dam was here long before the Absaroka-Beartooths were designated as wilderness. At any rate, most visitors have little difficulty enjoying the scenery and fresh air.

➤ **Fishing information:** There are a lot of fish willing to be caught near the trailhead at Emerald and West Rosebud lakes. Both lakes support hefty fish with brown trout, cutthroat trout, and whitefish all common. Rainbows are stocked in both lakes, to provide some additional excitement.

Mystic Lake supports a rainbow trout fishery that is great when the fish are feeding and frustrating when they are not, although the fickle rainbows found there can usually be coaxed. The rainbows can be counted on for a good workout. The stream up to Mystic is very steep and doesn't provide great habitat for fish, so save your effort for the lake.

12 GRANITE PEAK

General description:	A long, steep backpack to a traditional launching point for ascents of Montana's highest peak, Granite Peak. Strictly for experienced, well-conditioned hikers.
Total distance:	21 miles, plus the climb up Granite Peak.
Difficulty:	Difficult.
Special attractions:	A chance to view or climb Montana's highest mountain, 12,799-foot Granite Peak.
Topo maps:	USGS—Granite Peak and Alpine; RMS—Cooke City-Cutoff Mountain and Alpine-Mount Maurice.

Key points:

3.0 Mystic Lake Dam.
3.5 Junction with Phantom Creek Trail 17.
6.4 Froze-to-Death Divide.
10.5 Tempest Mountain.

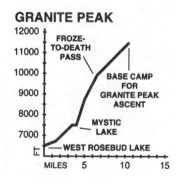

GRANITE PEAK

The trail: There is a choice of two trailheads for this hike—West Rosebud and East Rosebud. The West Rosebud is slightly more popular, mainly because its slightly shorter and cuts 400 feet of elevation gain off the approach to Granite Peak. Either trailhead leads to the same place—the saddle between Prairie View Mountain and Froze-to-Death Mountain. And whether coming from the east or west, the trails are for rugged types. Just reaching the saddle where the two trails meet is a climb of 3,500 feet from Mystic Lake or 3,900 from East Rosebud Lake.

Granite Peak, Montana's highest mountain and one of the most popular destinations in the Beartooths. Michael S. Sample photo.

Once at the saddle, turn southwest and follow a series of cairns around the north side of Froze-to-Death Mountain. The destination is an 11,600-foot plateau on the west edge of Tempest Mountain, 1.6 miles north of Granite Peak. Trekkers can camp here, but the area is way above timberline and gets heavy use, so please adhere strictly to no-trace camping ethics.

In past years, climbers have built rock shelters (rock walls about 3 feet high) on the west edge of Tempest Mountain to protect themselves from the strong winds that frequently blast the area. Each year, the Forest Service removed them because the area is designated wilderness and permanent structures are prohibited.

By the time it reaches the plateau, the trail has wandered more than 10 miles from the trailhead and gained more than 5,000 feet. It crosses timberline just before reaching the saddle. Rock, ice, and sky are the predominant elements. No plants or grasses can survive the climate and elevation at the plateau except hardy lichens.

There are some advantages to hiking and camping in such a forbidding place. The wind is so prevalent that few mosquitoes ever attempt takeoffs from ground zero. The bear danger is nil. And, of course, the high altitude grants superb views in all directions.

Along the west edge of the plateau leading up to Tempest, the view of Granite Peak is awesome. Granite buttresses rise almost vertically from Huckleberry Creek Canyon to form a broad wall nearly 0.5 mile wide. The north face is heavily etched with fissures running almost straight up between the buttresses. Granite Glacier clings to the center of the wall. At the top, a series of pinnacles builds from the west side up to the peak.

To those who are skilled in technical climbing, Granite is an easy ascent in good weather, but for those with little experience, it is dangerous. Probably the best advice is to go with someone who has the experience and proper equipment. Especially important is a good climbing rope for crossing several precipitous spots. The easiest approach is across the ridge that connects Granite to Tempest and then up the east side.

Check with the Forest Service for more information before attempting this climb. A special brochure is available for people interested in climbing Granite Peak. In recent years, not one summer has passed without mishaps and close calls, mostly due to bad judgment. One sobering concern is the extreme difficulty in rescuing an injured person from Granite.

People have tried this hike and climb at almost all times of the year, but August and early September are the most logical choices. Even then, sudden storms with sub-zero wind chills are a real possibility. Snow can fall anytime. And the thunderstorms around Granite Peak are legendary. Be prepared with warm and windproof clothing and preferably a shelter that will hold together and stay put in strong wind.

Whether or not you climb Granite, take the time to walk up to the top of Tempest. To the north and 2,000 feet below are Turgulse and Froze-to-Death lakes. On a clear day, you can see perhaps 100 miles out onto the Great Plains. And if you move a little east toward Mount Peal, you can look southwest over Granite Peak's shoulder to Mount Villard and Glacier Peak, both over 12,000 feet.

It should be no surprise that there is little wildlife at this altitude. Nearer the saddle, where grass and other hardy alpine plants eke out an existence, mountain goats are commonly seen. An occasional golden eagle soars through this country looking for marmots and pikas. Down closer to the trailheads, a few mule deer and black bears make their summer homes.

Those who come in from the East Rosebud trailhead may wish to take an alternate way back. From the east edge of the plateau to the west-northwest of Turgulse Lake, it's possible to descend into the bowl that holds Turgulse and hike past Froze-to-Death Lake and Phantom Lake. Then cross the hill back to rejoin the trail above Slough Lake. There is no trail for most of this route, and some investigating between Froze-to-Death and Phantom lakes may be necessary, but it is an interesting way out for the fit and adventurous. And high adventure is what this trip is all about in the first place.

13 ROSEBUD TO ROSEBUD

General description: A moderately long and difficult shuttle best suited for a long day trip.

Total distance: 13 miles.

Difficulty: Difficult.

Special attractions: Outstanding scenery.

Topo maps: USGS—Granite Peak and Alpine; RMS—Cooke City-Cutoff and Alpine-Mount Maurice.

Key points:

3.0   Mystic Lake Dam.

3.5   Junction with Phantom Creek Trail 17.

6.4   Froze-to-Death Plateau.

10.2   Slough Lake.

13.0   Phantom Creek Trailhead.

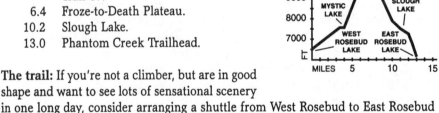

The trail: If you're not a climber, but are in good shape and want to see lots of sensational scenery in one long day, consider arranging a shuttle from West Rosebud to East Rosebud via the Phantom Creek Trail. Even better, talk some friends into a "trade keys" hike. This is a perfect route choice for such a plan. One party starts at West Rosebud and the other at East Rosebud. Meet on top of Froze-to-Death Plateau for lunch, trade vehicle keys, and drive each other's vehicle home.

The trading keys plan can be risky on long trips where folks want to stop to fish, climb, or partake in other activities that might lead off trail. In this case, most of the trip is above timberline and on a well-maintained trail. It's harder to miss each other. Whoever gets to the top of the plateau first should just relax and wait for the other party.

But be sure to pick a day with a good weather forecast. And roll out of bed early. This is a 13-mile day hike with lots of elevation gain—3,668 feet from West Rosebud and 3,932 feet from East Rosebud.

It would be difficult to argue which approach to the plateau is more scenic—definitely a win-win situation. It's about the same distance to an ideal rendezvous site on the top of Froze-to-Death Plateau.

This trip really doesn't offer much for overnight campsites. But camping is available at the upper end of Slough Lake on the East Rosebud side and along the east shore of Mystic Lake on the West Rosebud side. Those who do camp should practice strict no-trace camping techniques, as this area receives heavy use (mainly because of the fanatical interest in climbing Granite Peak).

➤ | **Fishing Information:** If doing this as a day hike, there won't be much time to get in any relaxed fishing. The rainbows are generally willing in Mystic Lake, as are the brookies along the lower stretches of Phantom Creek.

14 *ISLAND LAKE BASE CAMP*

General description:	One of the easiest base camps in the Beartooths, but with as many side attractions as any.
Total distance:	12 miles, plus side trips.
Difficulty:	Moderate, but with some difficult (optional) side trips.
Special attractions:	So much to see and do all within reach of base camp at Island Lake.
Topo maps:	USGS—Granite Peak; RMS—Cooke City-Cutoff Mountain.

Key points:

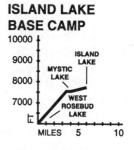

ISLAND LAKE BASE CAMP

3.0   Mystic Lake Dam.
3.5   Junction with Phantom Creek Trail 17.
5.7   Huckleberry Creek.
6.0   Island Lake.

The trail: The West Rosebud seems to have one disadvantage—or advantage, depending on your point of view. It's mostly suited for "just passing through."

The first three trips from this trailhead offer either day hikes or trips that pass through the West Rosebud for other destinations. Island Lake, however, affords a great chance to stay a few days and enjoy the many wonders of the West Rosebud Valley. It's especially suited for hikers who like to set up a base camp.

The first 3 miles up to the Mystic Lake Dam are described in the Mystic Lake trip. From this point, walk along the east shore of Mystic Lake on a well-maintained trail for about 2.5 miles. Then it's another 0.5 mile to Island Lake. Just before the end of the lake, the trail crosses Huckleberry Creek, which tumbles down from several lakes in the west shadow of Granite Peak. This is a big stream, but fortunately the Forest Service has built a sturdy bridge over it.

Overnighters must cross West Rosebud Creek to get to the choice campsites on the west side of the stream, and there's no bridge. In August or September, this won't be a problem. Cross easily on a logjam at the outlet of Island Lake. Early in the year at high water, however, this crossing could be more difficult. Lots of water comes down West Rosebud Creek. The Forest Service does not maintain the trail beyond a point just before West Rosebud Creek and Island Lake.

Just after West Rosebud Creek crossing is a huge flat area where many large parties could camp and still not bother each other.

The trail continues on to Silver Lake, which also offers base camp opportunities. but the trail is muddy and brushy, and the campsites at Silver Lake aren't as pleasant as those at Island Lake. Instead, consider visiting Silver Lake on a day trip from base camp. Another good possibility is a hike up Huckleberry Creek to Princess Lake and, for the well-conditioned, on to Avalanche Lake.

Two more options include a long trek to Grasshopper Glacier and a climb up to a series of lakes—Nugget, Beckworth, Frenco, Nemidji, and Weeluma—just west of Island Lake Base Camp. Only those in good shape and savvy in wilderness skills should attempt these side trips. It's possible, of course, to just hang around and explore the Island Lake and Mystic Lake country for a day or two and not miss out on anything.

➤ **Fishing information:** Starting at Island Lake anglers will begin to find an occasional cutthroat trout mixed in with the rainbow population. These have migrated down from Weeluma, Nemidji, Nugget, Beckworth, and Frenco lakes, all pure cutthroat fisheries. Silver Lake sports some nice-sized hybrid trout that are hard to catch, but worth the effort.

While many people use Trail 17 to access Granite Peak, a lesser-used alternative is up Huckleberry Creek. Huckleberry Lake supports a healthy rainbow population, while Avalanche and the Storm lakes above are stocked with willing cutthroats that grow above average in size and weight. Mountain goats frequent this basin, and although this route is a steeper approach to Granite Peak, the added aspect of great fishing may make the climb worth it.

WHERE TO GO FROM ISLAND LAKE

After arriving at base camp at Island Lake, most people want to spend a day or two exploring. Here's a list of suggested day trips rated for difficulty as follows: "Human" (easy for almost everyone, including children), "Semi-Human" (moderately difficult) or "Animal" (don't try it unless you're very fit and wilderness-wise). Also refer to more detailed rating information in the chapter, "Using this Guidebook."

Destination	Difficulty
Granite Peak	Animal
Froze-to-Death Plateau	Human
Silver Lake	Human
Princess Lake	Semi-Human
Avalanche Lake	Animal
Weeluma & Nemidji Lakes	Animal
Fenco, Nugget, & Beckworth Lakes	Animal
Star Lake	Animal
Grasshopper Glacier	Animal

TRAILHEAD 5
EAST ROSEBUD

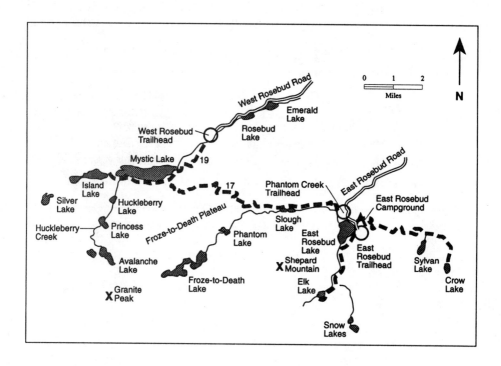

OVERVIEW

Many people who know the Beartooths say the East Rosebud is the most scenic valley of all. It's filled with lakes and waterfalls that would be major tourism attractions anywhere else. Here, there are so many, most don't even have names. The cutthroat-filled lakes bring a smile to any angler's face, and climbers love the place because of the endless array of rock faces. Families and friends frequently choose "The Beaten Path" for that long-planned wilderness adventure. Consequently, the East Rosebud Trailhead is probably the largest and most heavily used in the Beartooths.

Adding even more use to the area is the small community of summer homes called Alpine right at the trailhead. The summer homes extend up both sides of the lower sections of East Rosebud Lake, closing off much of the lake to public use.

The large trailhead has toilet facilities and plenty of room to park and turn around large horse trailers. It also has a campground.

FINDING THE TRAILHEAD

From Interstate 90 at Columbus, drive south 29 miles on Montana Highway 78 to Roscoe. Drive into this small ranching community, being careful not to stop at the Grizzly Bar—until the return trip of course, when you'll be really ready for the famous "Grizzly Burger." At the north end of Roscoe the road turns to gravel and goes about 14.5 miles to the East Rosebud Trailhead. About 7 miles from Roscoe the road crosses East Rosebud Creek and forks. Take a sharp right and continue south along the creek. The road is mostly gravel except a 4-mile paved section near the end.

Actually, there are three trailheads at East Rosebud Lake. Phantom Creek Trail 17 begins on the right (west) side of the road about 0.3 mile before the lake. This is a popular route to Froze-to-Death Plateau and Granite Peak. About 0.5 mile farther, as the road swings by Alpine and around the east side of the lake, turn left into East Rosebud Campground to reach the trailhead for Trail 13 to Sylvan Lake. Finally, Trail 15 up the East Rosebud ("The Beaten Path") begins at the end of the road about 0.25 mile past the campground.

CROSS REFERENCE

Be sure to read the "Rosebud to Rosebud" and "Granite Peak" trails described under the West Rosebud section. Both of these trails could be done from the Phantom Creek Trailhead on the East Rosebud side.

THE TRAILS

> Elk Lake
> The Beaten Path
> Sylvan Lake
> Slough Lake

15 ELK LAKE

General description: A moderately long but easy day trip.
Total distance: 6 miles.
Difficulty: Easy.
Topo maps: USGS—Alpine; RMS—Alpine-Mount Maurice.

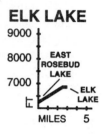

The trail: This trail covers the first 3.5 miles of the popular trans-Beartooth trail from East Rosebud to Cooke City, referred to in this book as "The Beaten Path." The trail is well-maintained and well-traveled. Expect to see lots of people.

The trail starts at the huge East Rosebud trailhead and goes through deep, unburned forest all the way to Elk Lake. From the trail there are several great views of 10,979-foot Shepard Mountain to the west and East Rosebud Creek as it tumbles down from the Beartooth Plateau.

Elk Lake is nestled in a forested pocket just below the point where the trail starts to traverse more rocky, open terrain. As a destination, it's best suited for day trips. The upper end of the lake has a pleasant spot for lunch.

Even though Elk Lake offers limited camping, a fair number of people spend the night here, mainly those who started too late in the day on their trans-Beartooth adventure.

The rocky, but well-constructed trail between Elk Lake and Rimrock Lake.

Rimrock Lake.

➤ **Fishing Information:** Elk Lake offers both cutthroat and brook trout fishing with the brook trout providing the largest portion of a possible dinner. Anglers day-hiking to Elk Lake should plan a couple of stops to fish in the creek. East Rosebud Lake holds some large brown trout, along with a mixed bag of brookies, rainbows, and cutthroats.

16 *THE BEATEN PATH*

General description: The most popular trans-Beartooth route.
Total distance: 26 miles, not counting side trips.
Difficulty: Long and strenuous, but not technically difficult or dangerous.
Special attractions: Perhaps the best opportunity to really experience the breadth and diversity of the Beartooths.
Topo maps: USGS—Alpine, Castle Mountain, and Fossil Lake; RMS—Alpine-Mount Maurice and Cooke City-Cutoff Mountain.

Key points:

3.0	Elk Lake.
6.0	Rimrock Lake.
7.0	Rainbow Lake.
9.0	Lake at Falls.
9.9	Big Park Lake.
11.8	Duggan Lake.
12.0	Impasse Falls.
12.8	Twin Outlets Lake.
14.0	Dewey Lake.
16.0	Fossil Lake.
16.8	East Rosebud/Clarks Fork Divide.
16.8	Gallatin/Custer National Forest boundary.
17.1	Windy Lake.
17.8	Skull Lake.
18.4	Bald Knob Lake.
18.8	Ouzel Lake.
20.0	Russell Lake.
22.0	Junction with trail to Fox Lake.
22.2	Junction with Crazy Lakes Trail No. 3.
23.0	Junction with Trail 566 to Rock Island Lake.
14.5	Kersey Lake.
26.0	Clarks Fork Trailhead, U.S. Highway 212.

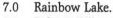

THE BEATEN PATH

The trail: This trip showcases all the beauty and austerity and emptiness and majesty of the Beartooths. It's a great introduction to the region's richness, diversity, and starkness, traveling through the lowest bottomlands and the highest plateaus. Along the way, the route skirts dozens of trout-filled lakes and stunning but unnamed waterfalls. It penetrates rich forests and wanders the treeless, lichen-covered Beartooth Plateau. This trail touches the true essence of the Beartooths.

This is the land of rushing water. Waterfalls and frothy, cascading streams are everywhere. There's no such scenery in Yellowstone National Park. Nonetheless, we should all be elated to have the park so near, because it sucks up all the people and leaves places like the East Rosebud for us.

Yet this trail receives relatively heavy use compared to other routes in the Beartooths. If there's such a thing as "The Beaten Path," the East Rosebud is it. Amazingly, however, The Beaten Path does not seem crowded. Even though hundreds of people may be somewhere along the 26-mile trail, most hikers would never know it. It's always a surprise to meet another party on the trail, and quiet spots to camp abound.

For uninterrupted solitude, and to really enjoy and experience the Beartooths, do make an effort to get *off* The Beaten Path. This trail has dozens of options for off-trail adventures—which is one reason the Beartooths can swallow up hundreds of people and leave the trail abandoned.

Don't take this trip lightly. It requires a minimum of four nights out, but avid explorers could stay two weeks and not see anything twice. This trail description

A scenic but unusually named area, Lake at Falls.

THE BEATEN PATH

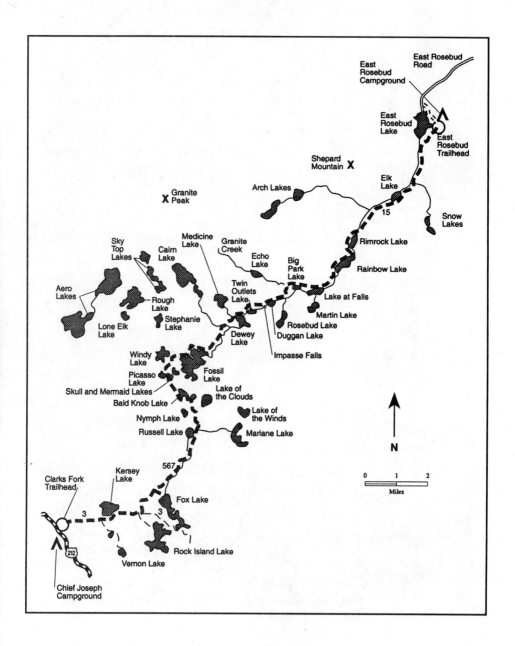

East Rosebud Road

East Rosebud Campground

East Rosebud Lake

East Rosebud Trailhead

Shepard Mountain X

Elk Lake

15

Snow Lakes

Arch Lakes

Granite Peak X

Rimrock Lake

Sky Top Lakes

Cairn Lake

Medicine Lake

Granite Creek

Echo Lake

Big Park Lake

Rainbow Lake

Aero Lakes

Rough Lake

Twin Outlets Lake

Lake at Falls

Martin Lake

Lone Elk Lake

Stephanie Lake

Rosebud Lake

Dewey Lake

Duggan Lake

Impasse Falls

Windy Lake

Picasso Lake

Fossil Lake

Skull and Mermaid Lakes

Lake of the Clouds

Bald Knob Lake

Nymph Lake

Lake of the Winds

Russell Lake

Mariane Lake

N

Kersey Lake

567

0   1   2
Miles

Clarks Fork Trailhead

3

Fox Lake

3

212

Rock Island Lake

Vernon Lake

Chief Joseph Campground

Fossil Lake.

assumes a minimum of four nights out.

It's also hard to make good time on this trail. There are simply too many distractions—too many scenic vistas, too many hungry trout, too many fields of juicy berries. Plan on traveling about a mile per hour slower than normal.

Also, be sure to plan this trip carefully. The first big issue is transportation. The best option is to arrange with friends or relatives to do the trip at the same time. Each party starts at opposite ends of the trail, meeting at a campsite midway along the trail. Spend a day or two together, then head out and drive each other's vehicles home. Or leave a vehicle at one end of the trip and drive around to the other trailhead, or arrange to be picked up.

Actually, less elevation is gained by starting this trip at the south end at the Clarks Fork Trailhead at 8,036 feet. However, since the north end is more accessible and scenic, more parties start from the East Rosebud Trailhead at 6,208 feet. Either way, the uphill climb really isn't severe; it's more of a gradual ascent most of the way. Perhaps the steepest section is between Elk Lake and Rimrock Lake.

The entire 26 miles of trail is well-maintained and easy to follow, so even a beginning backpacker can master it with ease. However, getting off The Beaten Path requires advanced wilderness skills.

The first 3 miles into Elk Lake are well-traveled and go by quickly. Expect to see lots of people on this popular stretch of trail. But every step of the way beyond Elk Lake is a step deeper and deeper into the wilderness, and it really seems like it. Elk Lake has a few campsites, but Rainbow Lake—7 miles in—is a better choice for the first night out if there's enough daylight left to get there.

Just after Elk Lake, the trail passes through an area where wild berries are as abundant as anywhere in the Beartooths, so browsers beware. Progress can slow to glacial speed. For about a mile, a kaleidoscope of berries beckons from trailside, with huge crops of most species found in the Beartooths in abundance, especially huckleberries, thimbleberries, and wild raspberries, all nicely ripe in mid-August.

From berry heaven, the trail breaks out of the forest and climbs about 800 feet through a monstrous rock field to Rimrock Lake. For a mile or so below the lake, East Rosebud Creek is little more than a long set of rapids. Apparently a big rockslide formed a natural dam and backed up Rimrock Lake. Take a rest on the rock field and look around at the trail and marvel at how it was constructed. Building a trail here was no small feat, especially negotiating the steep slopes around Rimrock Lake.

The trail crosses East Rosebud Creek on a sturdy wooden bridge at the outlet. Then it skirts above the west side of the lake, the tread expertly etched out of the rock face. After the climb to get here, camping at Rimrock Lake might seem like a good idea. But campsites are limited here, so it's better to drag on for another mile to Rainbow Lake for the first night out.

Both Rimrock and Rainbow lakes display a beautiful blue-green color (often called "glacier milk") indicative of a glacier-fed lake. Camping at Rainbow Lake affords a great view of Whirlpool Creek as it falls into the lake after tumbling down from Sundance Glacier on 12,408-foot Castle Rock Mountain.

The terrain at the upper end of Rainbow Lake flattens out and offers plenty of good campsites. Other parties probably will be camped here, but the area is big enough to provide ample solitude for all campers. Horse campers use this place heavily, but the Forest Service has required horses to stay above the trail, leaving several excellent campsites below the trail for backpackers only.

After the great scenery at Rimrock and Rainbow lakes, it might seem that it can't get much better. Guess again. Plan on lots of camera stops on the trip from Rainbow Lake to Fossil Lake.

Also watch for the mountain goats that inhabit this section of the East Rosebud drainage.

If the falls on Whirlpool Creek were impressive, the two falls from Martin Lake that drop into well-named Lake at Falls are awe inspiring. Yet another mile or so up the trail be prepared for perhaps the most astounding sight of the trip, massive Impasse Falls, which plunges about 100 feet into Duggan Lake. Travelers get great views of the torrent from both below and above as the trail switchbacks beside the falls.

From Impasse Falls, the trail goes by two more large, unnamed waterfalls before arriving at Twin Outlets Lake. And the short stretch between Twin Outlets Lake and Dewey Lake features another series of waterfalls.

With all this scenery (and all the film you'll put through your camera) on the second day of this trip, it's hard to hold a steady pace. Each person's mileage and time on the trail will vary widely. It's 9 miles from Rainbow Lake to Fossil Lake. Figuring four nights from trailhead to trailhead, there are two options for the second night's camp. Either camp somewhere along the trail or push on to Fossil Lake and stay two nights there.

From the standpoint of available campsites, it's slightly better to forge on to Fossil Lake. Even though the scenery is great along this stretch, it lacks a good selection of campsites. The most serviceable sites are at Big Park Lake, Twin Outlets Lake, or Dewey Lake, and along the stream above Big Park Lake. Lake at Falls and Duggan Lake offer virtually no campsites.

Twin Outlets Lake is just below timberline, and it's the last place the Forest Service allows campfires. Campfires are prohibited in the Fossil Lake area, which is at about 10,000 feet in elevation, but this should take nothing away from the grand experience of spending a few nights in the absolute core of the Beartooths.

One more choice for the second campsite is Echo Lake, which entails a 1-mile side trip. The trail breaks off to the west from the main trail above Big Park Lake and just before the bridge across Granite Creek. This isn't an official trail, but it's easy to follow. Watch for mountain goats on the slopes on the south side of Echo Lake.

Count on spending at least one night in the Fossil Lake area. Arriving fairly early on the third day allows extra time to search for that flawless, dream campsite. If you can't find that ideal campsite at Fossil, try nearby Windy, Bald Knob, or Mermaid lakes.

The Fossil Lake area is the beating heart of a great wilderness, and much of the spirit of this top-of-the-world environment seems to flow from it, just as East Rosebud Creek does. You'll really be missing something if you just pass through it.

From a five-star base camp here, a multitude of remarkable day trips await. Always keep a close eye on the weather, and head back to camp if a storm rolls in—as they often do in this high-elevation paradise. Try to rise early and cruise around in the mornings instead of the afternoons, which is when thunderstorms rip through the Beartooths on an almost daily basis. Figure on spending a full day just to walk the perimeter of Fossil Lake.

About halfway along the trail around octopus-like Fossil Lake, a huge cairn marks the divide between two drainages (East Rosebud Creek and the Clarks Fork of the Yellowstone River) and the boundary between the Custer and Gallatin national forests. Fossil Lake drains into the East Rosebud, and Windy Lake empties into the Clarks Fork. On the Forest Service maps, the trail numbers change from Trail 15 to Trail 567. This is also the place for cross-country hikers to break off the main trail and head over to Windy Lake, which can be seen off to the west. Windy Lake might be called Fizzle Lake on some maps, just as several other lakes in this area have different names on different maps. That's reason enough to bring a complete selection of maps on this trip.

Leaving Fossil Lake, the trail goes by Skull, Bald Knob, and Ouzel lakes before dipping below timberline on the way to Russell Lake. Russell is nicely located for the last night out. Camp at either the upper or lower end of Russell Lake. To reach the campsite at lower end, ford the stream, which gets seriously large as it slowly leaves the lake. Unfortunately, Russell Lake receives heavy use and shows it, so you might want to camp elsewhere. Other choices for the last night out would be Fox or Rock Island lakes. The trail to Fox isn't an official trail, but it's well-marked.

The trail from Russell Lake is probably the least attractive stretch of the trip, but most people would still rate it fairly high. For 6 miles, it passes through a dense lodgepole forest. The 1988 fires burned the section around Kersey Lake.

With luck, you'll come out on a hot day. Besides being the most scenic trailhead in the Beartooths, the Clarks Fork Trailhead offers the best swimming hole. Wearing a five-day accumulation of sweat and grime, most hikers feel an overpowering temptation to jump in. Don't fight it; just do it.

Fishing information: The Montana Department of Fish, Wildlife & Parks (DFWP) knows this is the most popular trail in the Beartooths and tries hard to complement this with a great fishery.

East Rosebud Lake houses a mixed bag of brown trout, brookies, rainbows, and cutthroat trout. The steep terrain keeps the browns from moving far upstream, but brookies, rainbows, and cutthroats, and even a few goldens survive in various places upstream in East Rosebud Creek. Goldens were stocked in several lakes along this trail in the 1950s, but they readily crossbreed with both rainbows and cutthroats. Unless you really know trout, the golden trout characteristics are difficult to see.

With the exception of Cairn and Billy lakes there are no brook trout above Elk Lake in this drainage. Rainbows dominate in Rimrock and Rainbow lakes, and cutthroat trout dominate in the lakes above Rainbow Lake. Because of its popularity, Fossil Lake is stocked frequently with cutts to keep the fishing hot, although they can be hard to find because they tend to school.

If you camp at Elk Lake, you might have time for a side trip up to Snow Lakes. These lakes hold some nice rainbows, but the tough climb up the east side of Snow Creek keeps all but the most determined anglers away.

Anglers who camp near Big Park Lake might want to reserve an entire day for climbing (and it truly is a climb) in to and out of Scat and Martin lakes. DFWP is trying to establish a pure golden trout fishery there, and it may be worth the climb.

Cairn Lake would also provide a worthwhile side trip for those camping near Dewey Lake. Cairn and Billy lakes both have brook trout well above average in size. The trout don't reproduce well here, allowing those remaining to grow larger. DFWP closely monitors these lakes—a downstream migration of brook trout would seriously harm the cutthroat/rainbow fishery down below. If you catch brookies below Billy Lake, notify DFWP.

Entering the Clarks Fork side of the pass near Fossil Lake, the fishing gets even better. There are a great many lakes in the Clarks Fork drainage, and this trail goes through the heart of this incredible fishery. Because of the easy access for horses, most of the lakes along the trail were stocked with brook trout in the first half of this century. The brookies tend to be on the smaller side but provide some great fishing, and an easy meal.

Just off the trail, Leo Lake, Lake of the Winds, and Lake of the Clouds host cutthroat trout, while Gallery Lake also has rainbows. Fox Lake is one of those places that few people stop at, and many more should. It sports larger than average brookies, nice rainbows, and an occasional grayling that works its way down from Cliff Lake.

As an experiment, DFWP has stocked lake trout in Kersey Lake to prey on the brook trout population. It is hoped that by reducing the number of brookies, the remaining ones will grow larger. At last check, this seems to be working.

GETTING OFF THE BEATEN PATH

To get the most out of an extended trans-Beartooth trip, try some off-trail excursions. Only those proficient with compass and topo map should attempt cross-country travel. The following list of side trips has been ranked as "Human" (easy for almost everybody, including children), "Semi-human" (moderately difficult) and "Animal" (don't try it unless you're very fit and wilderness wise). Refer to the chapter "Using this Guidebook" for more information on ratings.

Destination	Difficulty
Snow Lakes	Animal
Arch Lakes	Animal
Echo Lake	Human
Martin Lake	Animal
Medicine Lake	Animal
Around Fossil Lake	Human
Cairn Lake	Semi-human
Fizzle (Windy) Lake	Human
Basin (Picasso) Lake	Human
Fulcrum (Mermaid) Lake	Human
Lake of the Clouds	Semi-human
Nymph (Leo) Lake	Semi-human
Looking Glass (Stephanie) Lake	Semi-human
Rough Lake, Aero Lakes	Animal
Sky Top Lakes	Animal
Gallery Lake	Semi-human
Mariane Lake	Human
Lake of the Winds	Semi-Human
Fox Lake	Human
Rock Island Lake	Human
Vernon Lake	Human
Curl Lake	Human
Aquarius Lake	Animal

Sylvan Lake, home of the golden trout. Michael S. Sample photo.

17 *SYLVAN LAKE*

General description: A long, hard day trip or moderate overnighter.
Total distance: 10 miles.
Difficulty: Moderate.
Special attractions: One of the few easily accessible golden trout lakes in the Beartooths.
Topo maps: USGS—Alpine and Sylvan Lake; RMS—Alpine-Mount Maurice.

Key points:

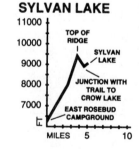

- 4.1   Top of ridge.
- 4.6   Junction with trail to Crow Lake.
- 5.0   Sylvan Lake.

The trail: The true beauty of Sylvan Lake lies beneath the surface. There swim the gorgeous, multi-colored golden trout in abundance. Biologists call the Sylvan Lake golden trout population one of the purest in the Beartooths, and they use the lake as a source of fish to plant in other lakes. However, even for the non-angler, this lake is worth the uphill trek.

Start up Trail 13 right from the East Rosebud Campground and gradually switchback up the steep slopes of the East Rosebud Plateau. It's 5 miles and almost completely uphill, but of course, the return trip is all downhill back to the trailhead. The trail is heavily used and well-maintained. It's also expertly designed so the climb doesn't seem so steep. The top of the ridge offers a fantastic view ("I climbed that!") of the East Rosebud Drainage, including East Rosebud Lake about 2,400 feet straight down.

On the ridge, the trail fades into a series of cairns for a few hundred yards, so be alert to stay on the trail. Also, don't miss the junction where the spur trail heads up to Sylvan Lake and Trail 13 continues on to Crow Lake. The junction is well-marked, but inattentive hikers could end up at the wrong lake.

Even though it's 10 miles total, Sylvan Lake is more suited for day trips. There is one campsite on a small plateau to the right just before the trail breaks over the last ridge into the lake basin. Camp here, however, and people will be walking by the front door of your tent. There are no campsites right at the lake. Sylvan Lake is at timberline, so please refrain from building a campfire.

An overnight stay at Sylvan does allow time for the short side trip over to Crow Lake, which probably surpasses Sylvan Lake for beauty, at least above the surface.

➤ | **Fishing information:** Anglers intent on pursuing the golden trout of Sylvan Lake should plan to spend the night. Goldens are shy and more easily caught in the morning and evening, precluding a day hike. The golden trout of Sylvan Lake reproduce readily, so don't worry about taking a few home, even if it's just to put one of these beauties on the wall. Anglers who make the trek to Crow Lake will find that the brook trout there are larger than average and are much easier to catch than the goldens at Sylvan.

---

19 *SLOUGH LAKE*

General description: A leisurely day trip.
Total distance: 4 miles.
Difficulty: Easy.
Topo maps: USGS—Alpine; RMS—Alpine-Mount Maurice.

The trail: This trail is perfectly suited for that leisurely, quiet day in the wilderness amid some great scenery.

The Phantom Creek Trailhead is on the right just before East Rosebud Lake. Trail 17 climbs, with gradual switchbacks, along Armstrong Creek (yes, it probably should be called the Armstrong Creek Trailhead) for about 2.5 miles before it breaks out of the forest into a great panorama highlighted by Hole-in-the-Wall Mountain to the south. Look ahead to see how the trail climbs up to Froze-to-Death Plateau.

The trail reaches Slough Lake (no relation to the Slough Creek that drains south

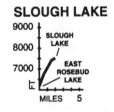

SLOUGH LAKE

from Boulder River country to the west) about 0.5 mile after the forest opens up. This is a gorgeous, glacier-carved cirque, and Slough Lake sits in the midst of it like a little pearl. Actually, there are two small lakes, and there's one campsite at the upper end of the second lake, for those inclined to stay overnight.

Even though this trail receives heavy use, few people take their time along here or even stop at Slough Lake. Most are rushing to the top of Froze-to-Death Plateau to climb Granite Peak. Lucky for the rest of us that they hurry right by this pastoral pond, a perfect spot to sit on a sunny day savoring the spirit of the wilderness.

➤ **Fishing information:** Slough Lake provides a good source of willing brookies for dinner, or for fun.

WEST FORK OF ROCK CREEK

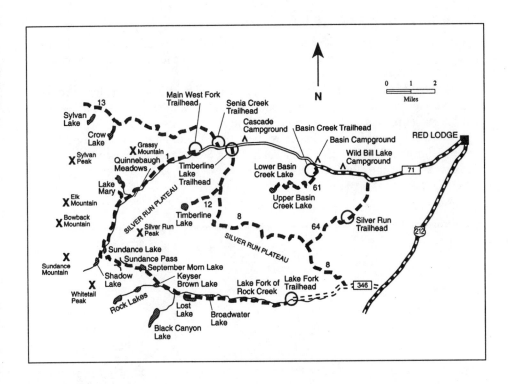

OVERVIEW

The West Fork of Rock Creek Road (Forest Road 71) actually boasts four separate trailheads, all in close proximity and included together in this section. Three vehicle campgrounds are also found in this area, and the lower valley has several residential developments. Since the road starts right in Red Lodge, the lower valley is almost the town's backyard wilderness.

The West Fork road is paved for the first 7 miles up to Basin Campground. This is a heavily used area, both for day trips and extended backcountry excursions. Fortunately, the area offers a wide range of trail choices and visitors tend to disperse. Trails rarely feel crowded.

FINDING THE TRAILHEAD

Turn west on the West Fork of Rock Creek Road (FR 71), which leaves U.S. Highway 212 on the south end of Red Lodge. After 2.7 miles, the road bends left and heads up the West Fork.

The first of four trailheads is Basin Creek, 7 miles from Red Lodge, followed by Timberline Lakes at 10.7 miles and Senia Creek at 12.5 miles. The last trailhead is at the end of the road, 14 miles from Red Lodge.

Three out of the four trailheads are well signed with large parking areas (big enough for small horse trailers) and toilet facilities. Senia Creek is not as well marked or developed as the other three trailheads.

On the Red Lodge Creek Plateau. Dick Krott photo.

CROSS REFERENCE

Refer to the "Rock Creek to Rock Creek" trip, which starts at the Lake Fork of Rock Creek Trailhead and ends at the West Fork of Rock Creek Trailhead. This trip could be done in reverse.

THE TRAILS

Basin Creek Lakes
Timberline Lakes
Silver Run Plateau
Lake Mary
Quinnebaugh Meadows
Crow Lake

19 BASIN CREEK LAKES

General description: An easy day hike well suited for families.
Total distance: 5 miles to lower lake, 8 miles to upper lake.
Difficulty: Easy.
Special attractions: A very accessible, safe trail, designated as a National Recreational Trail.
Topo maps: USGS—Bare Mountain; RMS—Alpine-Mount Maurice.

Key points:

0.0	Basin Creek Trailhead.
0.5	Basin Creek Falls.
2.5	Lower Basin Creek Lake.
4.0	Upper Basin Creek Lake.

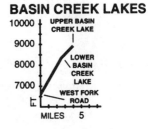

The trail: Basin Creek has been designated as a National Recreational Trail by the Forest Service, so not surprisingly, it's popular. It's so popular, in fact, that this is one of the few trails in the Beartooths restricted to hiking only—no horses are allowed until mid-September when the big game hunting seasons get underway.

Technically, Trail 61 to Basin Creek Lakes does not lie within the Absaroka-Beartooth Wilderness, but it's a wilderness trip by all other definitions. The trail is well-maintained, easy to follow, and ideal for family day trips for those who can handle the gradual, but steady, uphill gradient. The route crosses Basin Creek twice, but bridges keep your feet dry.

About 0.5 mile up the trail, listen for Basin Creek Falls tumbling down from above. Where the trail takes a sharp right, hikers can scramble up a short, undeveloped spur trail to get a closer look at the falls, which is well worth the short detour. The rest of the trail is hazard-free, but this short climb up to see the falls might be too hazardous for small children.

The trail passes through thick forest all the way. With so much of the Beartooths burned by the 1988 fires, this peaceful walk in the woods can be a real treat. The remains of past logging activity from the early 1900s are still visible along the way—but it's also apparent that nature is finally reclaiming the disturbed landscape.

Lower Basin Lake is one of those forest-lined mountain ponds with darkish, warm water that tends to be half-covered by lily pads. Upper Basin Lake is larger, deeper, and nestled in a picturesque mountain cirque.

Although better suited as a destination for day trips, the upper lake also offers a few potential campsites. There is enough firewood for a campfire.

➤ | **Fishing information:** While both of these lakes once supported brook trout populations, the lower lake suffered a freeze-out a few years back and currently has no fish. Since the brook trout in the stream and lake above will eventually work their way back down to Lower Basin, there is no immediate need to restock. Fishing in Upper Basin Lake is excellent for brook trout, and there has been some talk of introducing grayling.

20 *TIMBERLINE LAKE*

General description: A moderately long day trip or easy overnighter.
Total distance: 9 miles.
Difficulty: Easy.
Special attractions: The view from Timberline Lake.
Topo maps: USGS—Sylvan Peak and Bare Mountain; RMS—Alpine-Mount Maurice.

Key points:

0.0	Timberline Lakes Trailhead.
3.0	Junction with Beartrack Trail 8.
4.0	Lake Gertrude.
4.5	Timberline Lake.

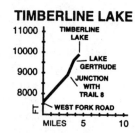

The trail: Similar to the nearby trail up Basin Creek, the trail to Timberline Lake passes through a forested environment. Here, however, the forest is more open and mature than along Basin Creek. As with almost all trails in the Custer National Forest section of the Absaroka-Beartooth Wilderness, this one is well maintained and marked.

The corridor to Timberline Lake was excluded from the Absaroka-Beartooth Wilderness. However, Lake Gertrude and Timberline Lake lie within the wilderness boundary, and current wilderness bills call for adding the corridor to the wilderness.

It's a short 3 miles to the junction with Beartrack Trail 8, which veers off to the left and heads up to Silver Run Plateau. Turn right and continue along Timberline

Creek. If you cross the stream here, you took a wrong turn.

After another mile or so, look for Lake Gertrude nestled in a forested pocket off to the right. This is a good spot to pause for a rest while enjoying Lake Gertrude, which also marks the boundary of the Absaroka-Beartooth Wilderness. Don't burn too much daylight here, however—Timberline Lake is only 0.5 mile farther and the basin is definitely worth exploring.

For an overnight trip, it's possible to camp near the inlet of Lake Gertrude, but most people will probably enjoy the night out more by going the extra 0.5 mile to Timberline Lake. At Timberline Lake, camp on the moraine on the east side of the lake or near the inlet.

The view from Timberline Lake is fantastic, especially to the south toward Timberline Glacier and 12,500-foot Silver Run Peak. Adventuresome hikers might want to try a side trip up to the glacier.

➤ | **Fishing information:** Both lakes along this trail have healthy populations of brook trout. The fish aren't large, but can probably be counted on to provide dinner. The small outlet ponds below Timberline Lake may prove an easier place to catch fish than the lake itself.

21 *SILVER RUN PLATEAU*

General description: A unusual but surprisingly beautiful overnighter or, for the very fit, a long day trip.
Total distance: 17 miles.
Difficulty: Difficult.
Special attractions: An extraordinarily scenic high plateau with a challenging trail to follow.
Topo maps: USGS—Sylvan Peak and Bare Mountain; RMS—Alpine-Mount Maurice.

Key points:
3.0   Junction with Beartrack Trail 8.
4.4   Silver Run Lake Basin.
5.1   Trail turns to string of cairns.
11.0   Junction with Trail 64.
14.5   End of Trail 64 turns into gravel road.
17.0   West Fork of Rock Creek Road 71.

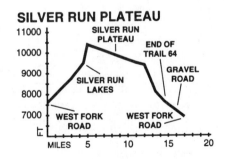

The trail: This is unconditionally one of the most remarkable and unusual trails in the Beartooths. It doesn't feature an endless string of lakes as do most trails here,

Arctic gentian, *a rare, pale green flower found in abundance on Silver Run Plateau.*
Michael S. Sample photo.

but most hikers will be too busy enjoying the trip to notice. Only the midsection of this trail is actually within the Absaroka-Beartooth Wilderness, but the entire trip seems unusually wild.

Weather is always important in the Beartooths, but it's especially critical on this trail. Double check the weather report before leaving home. A pair of nice sunny days is essential for this trip. Be sure to take an extra water bottle, as water is scarce, especially in later summer.

Another big issue on this trail is transportation. Arrange to be picked up or leave a vehicle (or bicycle) at the end of the trail to get back to the vehicle at the Timberline Lake Trailhead. The turn off to Silver Run Trail 64—the far end of this hike—is marked on the south side of the West Fork Road, about 2 miles past the turn off to Palisades Campground. The spur road to this trailhead can be traversed by any vehicle, but a high-clearance vehicle is better.

From the Timberline Lake Trailhead, hikers share the first 3 miles with everyone going to Timberline Lake. At the junction with Beartrack Trail 8, however, go left and cross Timberline Creek and head another mile along the east side of the creek to Silver Run Basin.

Since the tiny lakes in the Silver Run Basin aren't much of a fishery, the area doesn't get much use. However, the scenery equals any high-altitude basin in the Beartooths. Backpackers will probably want to spend their night out in the luxurious accommodations found in Silver Run Basin. It's definitely a room with a view. Camp almost anywhere in the basin. Campsites can also be found up on the plateau, but the only water would be small, snowmelt rivulets. Wherever you camp, follow strict no-trace practices to keep this area as pristine as it presently is. No campfires, please.

The trail is easy to follow up to the basin, but in the basin, it becomes difficult to find in places. As the trail leaves the basin and starts switchbacking up a steep slope to the plateau, it becomes clearly visible again. If you lose the trail in the basin, look ahead to see where it climbs up to the plateau.

Immediately after the last switchback on the edge of the plateau, the trail disappears, and nothing marks the way but a long string of cairns. Other trails in the Beartooths have short stretches of cairns, but in this case the cairns mark the way for about 7 miles. Fortunately, the cairns are well-placed, large, and unusually easy to follow.

The Silver Run Plateau is all above 10,000 feet and affords a fresh perspective of the Beartooths. It's nearly trackless, treeless, bugless, waterless, and peopleless, but none of these shortages detract from its raw beauty. For example, take a minute to look over your shoulder to the west for a view of 12,500-foot Silver Run Peak. Or look down at your feet to see the rare Arctic gentian. This is one of the few places in the Beartooths where this lovely, pale green flower is found in abundance.

Traveling from cairn to cairn, do a good deed and help keep the cairns maintained. If a cairn has collapsed, take the time to re-build it. When approaching a cairn, look for a rock or two that looks like it needs a new home, carry it the last few feet, and then use it to build up the cairn.

After following cairns for about 6 miles, watch for the junction with Silver Run Trail 64. Beartrack Trail 8 continues straight into the Lake Fork of Rock Creek. Instead, turn left on Silver Run Trail 64 and head down Silver Run Creek into the West Fork of Rock Creek.

After this junction, there's only another 0.5 mile or so of the long journey on Silver Run Plateau. Before dropping off the edge of plateau onto a normal, forested trail, glance backward for a last look at the plateau.

The trail drops rapidly into Silver Run Creek, so steeply that doing this trip in reverse would seem irresponsible. Stay on this trail for about 4 miles until it turns into the gravel road where you left a vehicle or are being picked up.

On the way down from the plateau, take note of "Stock Driveway" signs nailed on trees. This area, including the plateau, was once heavily grazed by sheep. Since then, the grazing allotment has been closed, mainly because of potential damage to this fragile environment.

➤ | **Fishing information:** The only real fishery along this route is found at one of the Silver Run Lakes. Only one of the five small lakes, the southern-most lake, contains fish (brookies).

22 *QUINNEBAUGH MEADOWS*

General description: A moderate day hike, easy overnighter, or base camp trip.
Total distance: 10 miles
Difficulty: Easy, except for a difficult side trip (optional).
Special attractions: An unusually large and beautiful mountain meadow.

Topo maps: USGS—Sylvan Peak and Bare Mountain;
RMS—Alpine-Mount Maurice

Key points:

1.3   Calamity Falls.
1.8   Sentinel Falls.
5.0   Junction with Lake Mary Trail and
      Quinnebaugh Meadows.

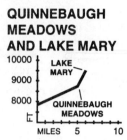

QUINNEBAUGH
MEADOWS
AND LAKE MARY

The trail: The trail, like others in this region, is well-maintained and marked. It closely follows the West Fork, not climbing any more than the stream drops in elevation as it powers its way out of the Beartooths. Most of the trail passes through a rich forest that gradually thins out as you progress up the drainage. In a few places, the forest opens up into small meadows with rewarding vistas of Elk Mountain and Bowback Mountain on the southern horizon near the terminus of the West Fork valley.

The trail passes close by Calamity Falls and Sentinel Falls. These cascades are reminders that the West Fork is not only a peaceful stream meandering out of the wilderness, but it can be a powerful force. Short spur trails lead to both falls for better views.

The West Fork broadens out and slows down just as the trail nears Quinnebaugh Meadows. Look for the sign for Lake Mary just after breaking out into the enormous mountain meadow.

Overnighters can set up camp almost anywhere in Quinnebaugh Meadows. It would, in fact, be difficult to not find a great campsite. In most campsites, there should be enough wood for a campfire. This is a popular place, so expect company. Fortunately, the meadow is large enough to accommodate several parties.

The extra dimension of Quinnebaugh Meadows is its attractiveness as a base camp. This site is perfect for someone who wants to camp in a lovely wilderness setting but doesn't want to carry a heavy pack very far—or up any big climbs. It's an easy 5 miles to get into the meadows, and that's 5 miles closer to many interesting destinations, mostly off-trail excursions. Strong hikers might be tempted to go 2 or 3 more miles past Quinnebaugh Meadows before setting up a base camp, but regrettably, the rest of the drainage offers much less attractive campsites than Quinnebaugh Meadows.

From this base camp, avid hikers could spend a week exploring the surrounding wilderness, taking a new route each day. Whether you're an angler, a climber, or simply out to see lots of really grand country, you won't be disappointed.

➤   **Fishing information:** Although the West Fork of Rock Creek is not highly productive, anglers can find a few trout in many stretches of this stream, The stream near Quinnebaugh Meadows is no exception. The best fishing, however, is found in various basin lakes 1,000 feet higher in elevation. With the exception of Lake Mary, none of these is easy to access, but all of them may be worth the trip.

A crude trail leads to Senal and Dude lakes between two bridges over the creek that drains them. It's a difficult side trip, but there are nice brookies and cutts in Senal, and pure cutts in Dude. Cutthroats are stocked in Dude on an eight-year cycle, last done in 1991.

Ship Lake Basin contains six lakes, all of which hold fish. The highest lake in Montana with fish is Marker Lake, and it has nice aggressive cutthroats, that are stocked on an eight-year cycle. Bowback, Kookoo, and Triangle lakes are also stocked on the eight-year cycle. The reference year is 1995 for all but Bowback which was last stocked in 1988. Ship Lake has easy-to-catch brookies, if the local cutts have stumped you.

On the main creek, Shadow, Sundance, and the Silt lakes are stocked with cutthroat trout, but these don't grow as well as those in the lakes above.

Many hikers use Sundance Pass as access to the Lake Fork of Rock Creek, where the first lake encountered is September Morn Lake. September Morn has an abundance of brookies.

WHERE TO GO FROM QUINNEBAUGH MEADOWS

Anybody who ventures off the trail in this area (or anywhere, for that matter) should be proficient with compass and topo map. The following destinations are ranked for difficulty, as follows: "Human" (almost anybody can do it), "Semi-human" (moderately difficult), or "Animal" (don't do it unless you're very fit and wilderness wise).

Destination	Difficulty
Lake Mary	Human
Crow Lake	Animal
Sundance Lake	Human
Sundance Pass	Human
Dude Lake	Animal
Shadow Lake	Human
Kookoo Lake	Animal
Ship Lake Basin	Animal
Marker Lake	Animal

Fishing at Lake Mary. Michael S. Sample photo.

23 *LAKE MARY*

General description:	A steep climb to a gorgeous mountain lake, well suited for a weekend overnight trip.
Total distance:	12 miles.
Difficulty:	Easy for the first 5 miles, very steep for the last mile.
Special attractions:	A special view of the entire West Fork of Rock Creek valley.
Topo maps:	USGS—Sylvan Peak and Bare Mountain; RMS— Alpine-Mount Maurice.

Key points:

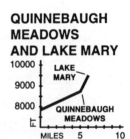

1.3	Calamity Falls.
1.8	Sentinel Falls.
5.0	Quinnebaugh Meadows.
5.1	Junction with Lake Mary Trail.
6.0	Lake Mary.

The trail: The first 5 miles of the trail into Lake Mary is described under the Quinnebaugh Meadows trip.

This hike comes in two distinct parts. The first half is the first 5 miles, and the second half is the last mile. Those carrying a big pack can plan on two hours for the first 5 miles and two hours for the last mile.

Stroll on up to Quinnebaugh Meadows. Enjoy a nice long rest and relish the picturesque openness of the meadow. Then take a deep breath before starting the ascent. The trail is well-constructed with frequent switchbacks to minimize the grade, but it's still a grind. It climbs 1,200 feet in only 1 mile. Even though Lake Mary sits at 9,900 feet, the trail doesn't break out of the forest until just before the lake.

The good news is that Lake Mary is worth the effort. There are campsites on either side of Lake Mary, which is actually two lakes. Especially agile hikers can cross the shallow section separating the lakes with some precarious rock-hopping. Since Lake Mary is above timberline, please refrain from building campfires. And of course, if the climb is too intimidating with a pack, there is the option of pitching camp in Quinnebaugh Meadows and hiking up to the lake with just a day pack.

➤ **Fishing information:** The West Fork of Rock Creek is characterized by beautiful cascades and sparkling pools, all of which are exceptionally photogenic, but most of which provide few fish. The very cold water, restricted sunlight, and rapid current make life difficult for fish. Cutthroat trout are more able to cope with these factors, although anglers will also find a few brook trout.

Lake Mary harbors a nice population of brook trout, comparable to those found elsewhere in the Beartooths. Count on them for dinner.

The route to Lake Mary from Crow Lake. Don't take the obvious pass to the right. Instead, go over the ridge at about 10 o'clock. Dick Krott photo.

Crow Lake.

24 *CROW LAKE*

General description: An overnighter into a seldom visited area.
Total distance: 14 miles.
Difficulty: Moderate, except for the difficult trip to Lake Mary (optional).
Topo maps: USGS—Sylvan Peak and Bare Mountain; RMS—Alpine-Mount Maurice.

Key points:

0.0	Senia Creek Trailhead.
4.2	Junction cutoff to Trail 14 down West Red Lodge Creek.
6.5	Junction with Crow Lake Trail.
7.0	Crow Lake.

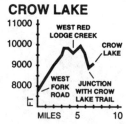

The trail: This trail starts at the Senia Creek Trailhead about 1 mile before the end of the West Fork Road. This is the smallest, least-used trailhead in the West Fork area, but it's still easy to find and well-maintained with a small parking area. Before starting up Trail 13, make sure the water bottles are full. It's a long, steep 4 miles until they can be re-filled.

From the trailhead, the route switchbacks up to the Red Lodge Creek Plateau, climbing about 1,800 feet in 2.6 miles. At that point (at higher than 9,500 feet), the trail breaks out of the timber onto the plateau. The first part of this trail is a grind, but after catching your breath, you'll find the scenic vistas from this high-altitude plateau a fitting reward.

The trail up to the plateau is well-defined, but after 0.5 mile or so on the plateau it fades away in places. Stay alert and follow cairns to find the route. Try to stay on the trail to protect the fragile vegetation clinging to existence in this austere environment.

After about 1 mile on the plateau, the trail reaches its highest point on this trip (9,980 feet) just before descending about 500 feet into West Red Lodge Creek. This is a great place to stop for a lengthy rest and to refill any empty water bottles.

About 0.25 mile after crossing the creek, there's a well-signed junction with a trail cutting off to the northwest and joining up with Trail 14 down West Red Lodge Creek. Turn left (west), staying on Trail 13.

After the junction, Trail 13 descends over the course of 1.8 miles to Hellroaring Creek. The first 0.5 mile or so is still above timberline. Just off the plateau and into the timber, watch for a glimpse of Crow Lake to the southwest. The trail soon crosses Hellroaring Creek and meets the trail to Crow Lake. Trail 13 keeps on heading west to Sylvan Lake. To get to Crow Lake, turn left (south) and follow the stream about 0.5 mile up to the lake.

There are campsites at the outlet. Those who still have some energy, however, might want to carefully cross the stream at the outlet and follow an angler's trail along the east side of the lake to a better campsite on the west side of the inlet.

Crow Lake doesn't get as many visitors as some lakes in the Beartooths, but that's changing. In the past few years, the lake has seen more use, especially from backcountry horsemen. There is, of course, a good reason for the new-found popularity. Crow Lake is well worth the trip. It lies in a beautiful forested pocket with several unnamed crags to the south, giving the lake a panoramic backdrop.

A base camp at Crow Lake allows hikers to day hike to Sylvan Lake, about 1.8 miles west on Trail 13. Head back down along Hellroaring Creek to the junction with Trail 13, turn left (west), and go about 1 mile. Just after crossing the outlet stream, the trail up to Sylvan Lake takes off to the left (south).

For a little adventure and to avoid backtracking to the Senia Trailhead, consider going over the ridge south of Crow Lake to drop into Lake Mary. Then follow Trail 1 out the West Fork back to the main West Fork Trailhead at the end of the road. This requires a 1-mile walk down the road to get to your vehicle at the Senia Creek Trailhead.

The off-trail section (about 2 miles) between Crow Lake and Lake Mary covers some rough country. This should only be attempted by those capable of navigating with compass and topo map. Also, be wary of what looks like the easiest route from the lake, a low pass to the right. Instead, check the topo map carefully before leaving Crow Lake and you'll see the best route is to the east over a ridge that looks more difficult than the other route, but really isn't. The last 0.5 mile into the Lake Mary basin goes through a pile of oversized rocks, so go slowly and carefully.

Taking the off-trail section makes a nice loop out of the trip. Camp the second night at Lake Mary, leaving an easy 6 miles for the last day.

➤ **Fishing information:** Crow Lake is not as popular a place as some lakes, and the brook trout found here are larger than average. Also make a fishing expedition over to Sylvan Lake if you have time. It holds a thriving golden trout population.

LAKE FORK OF ROCK CREEK

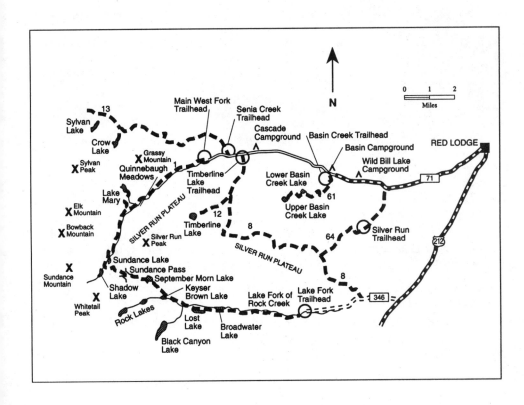

Sylvan Lake

13

Crow Lake

X Grassy Mountain

X Sylvan Peak

Quinnebaugh Meadows

Main West Fork Trailhead

Senia Creek Trailhead

Cascade Campground

Basin Creek Trailhead

RED LODGE

Basin Campground

Wild Bill Lake Campground

71

1

Timberline Lake Trailhead

Lower Basin Creek Lake

Lake Mary

SILVER RUN PLATEAU

Upper Basin Creek Lake

61

X Elk Mountain

12

Timberline Lake

8

64

Silver Run Trailhead

212

X Bowback Mountain

X Silver Run Peak

SILVER RUN PLATEAU

Sundance Lake

Sundance Pass

September Morn Lake

8

X Sundance Mountain

Shadow Lake

Keyser Brown Lake

Lake Fork of Rock Creek

Lake Fork Trailhead

346

X Whitetail Peak

Rock Lakes

Lost Lake

Broadwater Lake

Black Canyon Lake

N

0   1   2
Miles

The Lake Fork of Rock Creek with Thunder Mountain as a backdrop. Michael S. Sample photo.

OVERVIEW

The Lake Fork of Rock Creek area is similar to the West Fork, just to the north. Both areas are easily accessible from Red Lodge and receive lots of use. This high level of use in the Lake Fork may be even more obvious because everybody uses the same trail. In the West Fork, multiple trails tend to disperse the use.

FINDING THE TRAILHEAD

From Red Lodge drive southwest for about 10 miles on U.S. Highway 212. Turn west at the well-marked road up the Lake Fork of Rock Creek. A short, paved road leads to a turnaround and the trailhead.

THE TRAILS

Broadwater Lake
Rock Creek to Rock Creek

25 BROADWATER LAKE

General description: An easy day trip.
Total distance: 7 miles.
Difficulty: Easy.
Special attractions: Early in the year, watch for waterfalls cascading off the high plateau from the south.
Topo maps: USGS—Black Pyramid Mountain; RMS—Alpine-Mount Maurice.

The trail: From the trailhead, immediately cross a bridge over the Lake Fork of Rock Creek, turn right (west), and head upstream along the Lake Fork. The trail stays close to the stream all the way.

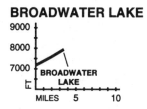

The trail is easy to follow, well-maintained, hazard-free, and usually dry. Plus, there are no steep hills to climb. The trail stays on the south side of the stream the entire way to Broadwater Lake, so there are no fords.

All of these advantages make this trip near-perfect for an easy day hike with children. Perhaps the best part of the trip into Broadwater Lake is constantly being

Medicine Mountain and the headwaters of the West Fork of Rock Creek. Michael S. Sample photo.

near a clean, natural mountain stream. Hikers can stop at dozens of places and just sit back against a tree, relax, and soak in the sound of the rushing water.

Along the way, watch for water ouzels playing in the blue-green waters of the Lake Fork. Also, expect to see lots of wildflowers along the stream.

Broadwater Lake is beautiful, but not well-named. It's not really a lake at all, but a long "glide" where the stream widens and slows for a few moments before hurrying out of the mountains.

There aren't really any good campsites in the area, so it's best to consider this a nice day trip.

> | **Fishing information:** Like the West Fork, the Lake Fork of Rock Creek is exceptionally photogenic, but it supports fewer fish than might be expected. The cold water, restricted sunlight, and fast current don't make life easy for fish. The Lake Fork supports both cutthroat and brook trout, but with some exceptions the numbers are not high. Fish concentrate in the slower sections of the stream, and Broadwater Lake is one of these.

25 ROCK CREEK TO ROCK CREEK

General description:	A fairly rugged, two- or three-day hike for experienced hikers.
Total distance:	21 miles, not counting side trips.
Difficulty:	Difficult.
Special attractions:	Spectacular mountain scenery, especially the view from Sundance Pass.
Topo maps:	USGS—Black Pyramid Mountain, Silver Run Peak, and Sylvan Peak; RMS—Alpine-Mount Maurice.

Key points:

3.5 Broadwater Lake.
5.0 Trail to Lost Lake.
5.2 Trail to Black Canyon Lake.
6.5 Turn to Keyser Brown Lake.
8.5 September Morn Lake.
11.3 Sundance Pass.
13.0 West Fork of Rock Creek.
13.5 Sundance Lake.
15.9 Junction with trail to Lake Mary.
16.0 Quinnebaugh Meadows.
21.0 West Fork Trailhead.

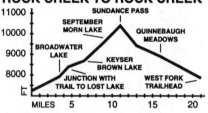

ROCK CREEK TO ROCK CREEK

Lost Lake. Michael S. Sample photo.

The trail: This well-maintained and heavily used trail is not only one of the most scenic in the Beartooths, but it's only a short drive from the Billings area.

This trail offers absolutely spectacular scenery. From Sundance Pass, for example, vistas include 12,000-foot mountains such as 12,548-foot Whitetail Peak, and the Beartooth Plateau, a huge mass of contiguous land above 10,000 feet. Hikers are also treated to views of glaciers and obvious results of glaciation, exposed Precambrian rock, and waterfalls. And watch for mountain goats, deer, golden eagles, and gyrfalcons. Goats are frequently seen from First and Second Rock lakes.

This is a fairly difficult, 21-mile shuttle trip that ends on the West Fork of Rock Creek just south of Red Lodge. Arrange to be picked up at the trailhead at the end of the West Fork of Rock Creek Road (Forest Road 71) or leave a vehicle there. An alternative is to have friends or relatives start at the other end of the trail, meet on Sundance Pass, and trade keys.

Plan to do this trip no earlier in the year than July 15. Sundance Pass usually isn't snow-free until then. This delay also avoids the peak season for mosquitoes and no-see-ums, which can be quite bad in this area, especially on the West Fork side.

The route gains 3,900 feet in elevation from beginning to end. Although nicely suited to a three-day/two-night trip, the route also offers many scenic side trips. Plan an extra day or two in the backcountry for exploring these.

The main route passes by three lakes—Keyser Brown, September Morn, and Sundance—but several others can be reached with short side trips. One of these is Lost Lake, which is a 0.25-mile climb from the main trail. This is a very heavily used lake, and it shows it. There are campsites here, but consider staying somewhere else that hasn't been trampled so much. The trail to Lost Lake leaves the main trail on the left, 5 miles from the trailhead or about 200 yards before the bridge over the Lake Fork of Rock Creek.

Another lake-bound trail departs from the main trail immediately before the same bridge. The unofficial trail to Black Canyon Lake scrambles uphill to the left also. Black Canyon Lake lies just below Grasshopper Glacier. The undeveloped trail to Black Canyon Lake is a rough but short hike of about 1.5 miles. Part of the route traverses rock talus with no trail, and there is a steep climb near the lake. The hike to Black Canyon is probably too tough for small children or poorly conditioned hikers. There is almost no place to camp at this high, rugged lake, and it's usually very windy at Black Canyon during midday.

The main trail continues west along the Lake Fork another mile to Keyser Brown Lake, about 7 miles from the trailhead. To do this trip in three days and two nights, plan to start early and spend first night at Keyser Brown. Although the wood supply is ample enough around Keyser Brown, this is one of the most heavily used campsites in the Beartooths. Please consider doing without a campfire here.

The lake is about 0.25 mile to the left (southwest), so watch carefully for the side trail. This is an official trail, and it's signed. The lake itself comes into view from the main trail, but if you can see it you've missed the junction and need to backtrack about 200 yards to the trail to the lake. An angler's trail leads south from the far end of Keyser Brown to First and Second Rock lakes. This side trip involves some difficult boulder-hopping.

For another campsite option, continue 1.5 miles up the main trail to September

Quinnebaugh Meadows in the West Fork of Rock Creek. Michael S. Sample photo.

Fishing at Black Canyon Lake. Michael S. Sample photo.

Morn Lake. The campsite selection is much more limited here than at Keyser Brown, but it is closer to Sundance Pass.

Get a good night's sleep and a hearty breakfast before starting the second day. From Keyser Brown it's a 1,660-foot climb to the top of Sundance Pass. The scenery is so incredible, however, that hikers might not notice how much work it is getting to the top. To the north and east stretch the twin lobes of the Silver Run Plateau, rising to their apex at 12,500-foot Silver Run Peak. Directly south of the pass, 11,647-foot Mount Lockhart partially shields the pyramid of 12,548-foot Whitetail Peak.

Coming down from Sundance Pass into the West Fork won't take long. A series of switchbacks drop about 1,000 feet in 1 mile or so to a bridge over the headwaters of the West Fork. Remember to carry extra water on this stretch—it is scarce on the pass.

Although there are campsites in a meadow about 0.25 mile down the trail from the Sundance Bridge, Quinnebaugh Meadows is probably the best choice for the second night out. It offers plenty of excellent campsites, and there's enough downed wood for a campfire. It's a long 8 miles from Keyser Brown to Quinnebaugh Meadows, but there aren't many good campsites between September Morn Lake and Quinnebaugh Meadows. Camping at the meadows leaves an easy 5 miles for the last day out. It might also allow enough time for a side trip up to Lake Mary or Dude Lake. Dude Lake is 1 mile west via a rough, steep trail from Quinnebaugh Meadows. And there's a steep but good trail from Quinnebaugh Meadows to Lake Mary. Some people use the saddle to the north of Lake Mary as a cross-country route to Crow, Sylvan, and East Rosebud lakes.

The final day of hiking follows the trail along the north bank of the West Fork all the way to the trailhead. Sentinel and Calamity falls both offer good places to drop the pack and relax.

Both the Lake Fork and the West Fork are probably used as heavily as any wild area in Montana. Consequently, the Forest Service has rangers out enforcing several protective regulations. These special regulations are listed at a sign on the trailhead. Be sure to read them carefully, and then, of course, obey them. They are necessary to protect these fragile environs.

This trip also works well in reverse. In fact, starting from the West Fork results in about 600 feet less overall elevation gain. However, Sundance Pass is tougher to climb from the West Fork side.

➤ **Fishing information:** The lakes found along the Lake Fork provide some of the easiest fishing in the Beartooths. Anglers will find plenty of hungry brookies in September Morn, Keyser Brown, and First and Second Rock lakes. Overnight campers can count on these lakes to supply dinner. Keyser Brown and Second Rock Lakes also support healthy cutthroat fisheries.

For those with something other than brook trout on their mind, Lost Lake supports a few cutthroat trout of surprising size. Grayling have also been planted in Lost Lake, and they grow large as well.

The scramble up to Black Canyon Lake rewards anglers with plenty of cut-throats near the glacial moraine that blocks the outlet. While this lake once grew exceptionally large fish, a probable change in food organisms, caused by the fish themselves, now keeps them in the slightly above-average range. This lake offers the best chance for catching a 15-inch or larger trout in the Lake Fork drainage.

From the crest of Sundance Pass, look to the lakes in the high basin across the West Fork to the northwest. Ship Lake is the largest of these. There are plenty of fish in these waters for hikers who don't mind climbing up the other side of the valley after coming down Sundance Pass. Refer to the Quinnebaugh Meadows trip for more information.

TRAILHEAD 8
ROCK CREEK

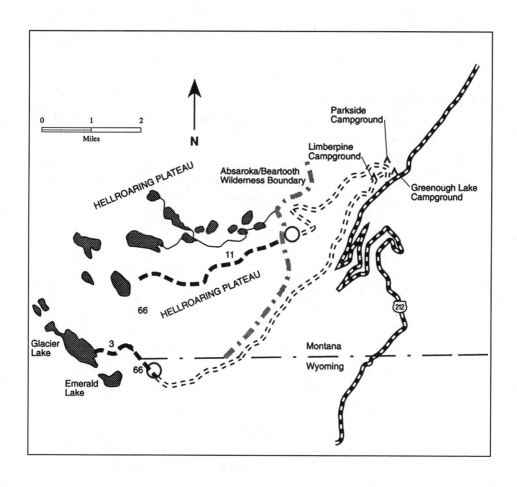

OVERVIEW

The Rock Creek area is the last stop before driving up the world-famous switchbacks to the top of Beartooth Pass and into Wyoming. Actually, there are two trailheads (Glacier Lake and Hellroaring) in the area, both accessed from the Forest Service campgrounds at the base of Beartooth Pass. Day hikers can camp at one of the three vehicle campgrounds and go to Hellroaring Lakes and Glacier Lake on extended one-day outings.

A high-clearance vehicle is needed to get to the trailheads. Snow usually blocks these gravel roads until July.

The trails in this area are great for learning to explore the high country with a topo map and compass, and they are especially well-suited for hikers who aren't in animal-like physical condition. Many lakes and other scenic areas can be reached within a few miles of each trailhead. The climbs can be steep, but not extended.

FINDING THE TRAILHEAD

Drive south from Red Lodge on U.S. Highway 212 for about 12 miles. Watch for a well-marked turnoff on the right (west) at Hellroaring Creek to three Forest Service campgrounds. This road enters the campground maze, but everything is well-signed. The roads to the two trailheads start immediately after a bridge across from the entrance to Limberpine Campground. Note the specific instructions in the two trail descriptions for more details on how to get to the trailheads.

THE TRAILS

Glacier Lake
Hellroaring Lakes

27 GLACIER LAKE

General description: A steep but short day trip or overnighter.
Total distance: 4 miles, plus side trips.
Difficulty: Moderately strenuous but short to Glacier Lake. Some side trips and exploring can be difficult.
Special attractions: A spectacular area accessible with a short hike.
Topo maps: USGS—Beartooth Butte and Silver Run Peak; RMS—Alpine-Mount Maurice and Wyoming Beartooths.

The trail: Although this route could be done as an overnighter, the Glacier Lake area seems nicely suited to a long day of exploring, fishing, photographing, and simply enjoying high-elevation majestic vistas. It's easily accessible by a 2-mile trail. The Forest Service has restricted stock use on this trail due to hazardous conditions for horses.

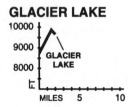

Glacier Lake. Michael S. Sample photo.

To get to the Glacier Lake trailhead, turn left (southwest) on the clearly signed gravel road just after crossing the bridge by the entrance to Limberpine Campground. Once on the correct road, there's no chance of getting off it because there are no other forks or spur roads. It's a long, slow 8 miles to the trailhead. Most of the road can be traversed by a passenger car, but a high-clearance vehicle is essential for the last 0.5 mile or so. A Weather Bureau Precipitation Gauge stands at the trailhead, and Trail 3 to Glacier Lake is well signed.

The trail to Glacier Lake is short but very steep. The trailhead is at 8,680 feet and the lake is at 9,702 feet, but the route actually climbs more than the difference (1,022 feet) in the 2 miles to Glacier Lake. That's because there's a ridge in the middle that's about 800 feet higher than the lake.

After climbing for about 0.5 mile, the trail crosses Moon Creek on a bridge. After Moon Creek, the trail gets even steeper—and the higher it goes, the better the scenery gets.

Shortly after Moon Creek, a faint, unofficial trail veers off to the north to Moon Lake and Shelf Lake. Turn left (west) and stay on what is obviously the main trail. For most of the way, the trail is rough and rock-studded, but it remains easy to follow and without hazards.

Once atop the ridge, cross some rock shelves on the way down to massive Glacier Lake. Even though the lake sits at 9,702 feet (above timberline), some large trees stand along the shoreline.

The trail reaches the lake at a small dam built long ago to increase the depth of Glacier Lake. A faint trail heads off to the right and goes about halfway around the lake. After a large point jutting out into the lake, the trail degenerates into a series of boulder fields and talus slopes. Watch for the amazing numbers of pikas that

Camping at Emerald Lake. Michael S. Sample photo.

inhabit the area.

Bearing right along the north shore of the lake affords views of Triangle Lake and access to Mountain Sheep Lake and Mountain Goat Lake at the head of the basin. All of the potential campsites along the north shore of Glacier Lake are cramped and marginal at best and probably too close to the lake.

Bearing left and across the dam around the south shore of the lake leads directly to Little Glacier Lake, a small jewel just barely separated from Glacier Lake. Continuing south on this trail over a small ridge treats wanderers to the sight of lovely Emerald Lake. For those planning to stay overnight, there are several quality campsites on the north side of Emerald Lake. The south side of the lake is spectacularly steep. This is high alpine country, so please resist the temptation to have a campfire.

Anglers must be sure to keep track of which state you're in, and make sure you have the right license. The state line goes right through Glacier Lake. Little Glacier and Emerald lakes are in Wyoming.

Because of topography, Glacier Lake tends to become remarkably windy during mid-day, so try to arrive early to catch the scenery before the winds start ripping through this valley. Emerald Lake is not quite as windy.

➤ **Fishing information:** The ice-cold water, high canyon walls, and swift-running water make Rock Creek extremely attractive to look at, but these conditions also make life hard for fish. Rock Creek is home to small populations of cutthroat and brook trout. Fish concentrate in the slower water, so look for good holding places out of the current. The main fork of Rock Creek winds in and out of Wyoming and Montana, so anglers need to know which state they're in and have the appropriate license.

Glacier Lake supports cutthroat and brook trout, both of which grow to above-average size. The fish tend to school, with cutthroats working rocky shorelines, so anglers should work the shoreline as well. When water levels are high, water flows between Glacier and Little Glacier lakes, so the fishery is the same in both. But the fish are easier to find in Little Glacier. Emerald Lake supports both cutts and brookies as well, though slightly smaller than those in Glacier.

Plan on seeing other anglers. The tough hike around Glacier Lake probably spreads out the competition. Cutts are stocked in Mountain Goat Lake and work their way down to Mountain Sheep Lake. Count on more fish in the upper lake and larger ones in the lower.

Fewer hikers go into Moon and Shelf lakes, as the trail seems steeper and longer than it is. Shelf Lake harbors hefty brookies, while Moon grows above average cutts.

Mountain Sheep Lake. Michael S. Sample photo.

Mountain Goat Lake. Michael S. Sample photo.

General description: A short, mostly off-trail trip into a high-elevation basin filled with lakes, best suited for day hiking.

Total distance: 4 to 8 miles, depending on how much exploring you do.

Difficulty: Moderate to difficult.

Special attractions: So much to see on such a short hike.

Topo maps: USGS—Black Pyramid Mountain; RMS—Alpine-Mount Maurice.

The trail: After driving over the bridge across from the entrance to Limberpine Campground take a short jog to the right on a well-signed road and start switchbacking up the ridge. The rocky road to the Hellroaring Trailhead climbs up a steep slope for about 6 miles. A high-clearance vehicle is needed to get over the sharp rocks and around the tight switchbacks. The last 0.25 mile to the trailhead gets very rough. The road ends on the edge of Hellroaring Plateau.

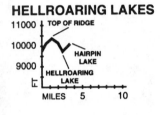

From the trailhead, follow an old, closed-off jeep road about 1 mile along the Hellroaring Plateau. Lower Hellroaring Lakes are soon visible in the valley off to right (north). You are better off continuing on along the plateau instead of going down to the lakes from this point. If you drop off too early, the terrain gets very steep and it's a fight through a maze of alpine willows and small streams.

Instead, continue along the plateau for another 0.5 mile or so. The scenery is worth it. Wander over to the south edge of the plateau on the left to see the main fork of Rock Creek.

At about the 1.5-mile mark and just before a huge snowbank on the right (northwest), head down to the lakes. Take a close look at the topo map before dropping off the plateau and keep the map handy until you climb back out of the basin.

The climb down to the lakes is more gradual from this point. Watch for game trails on the way down, but be prepared for essentially off-trail hiking. Once at the lakes, the hiking is much easier. There are fairly well-defined angler's trails between the lakes.

This is a heavenly basin filled with lakes, mostly above 10,000 feet. Hairpin Lake, for example, is definitely worth seeing. It has a series of beautiful bays, and a waterfall plunges into the lake from the northwest. There's plenty of grand places to explore and all within a short distance.

The basin is best suited for an extended day hike, but a few people camp there. The best choice for a campsite is around one of the lower lakes where there are more level spots and trees to break the wind. This is alpine country, so please don't burn up the aesthetic wood supply by using it for campfires.

After a few hours exploring the basin, climb back up to the plateau and back to your vehicle. To make a short loop out of the trip, hike down to the lower lakes and then up to the plateau. Bear in mind that the climb back to the plateau from the lower basin is tough. It's better to retrace your steps up the valley and then take the more gradual climb to the plateau just east of the large snowbank. Another short loop can be made by heading west to Sliderock Lake and then climbing back to the plateau on the west side of the snowbank.

While exploring the basin, watch the weather. It's all too easy—and dangerous—to get caught on the plateau by one of the severe thunderstorms that often roll through here in the afternoon.

➤ **Fishing information:** The Hellroaring Lakes number 13, which is almost the number of fishing opportunities found in this basin. Three lakes are fishless, and please leave them that way. If you prepare for mosquitoes, the lower lakes are the perfect place to take your son or daughter for their first mountain backpacking trip. Each small lake has its own personality, and most support brook trout and cutthroat trout, both of which are willing to be caught. The trees here provide cover from the wind and a visual break from the rocky terrain above.

When you're tired of catching the numerous smaller trout in the lower lakes, head up the drainage. Hairpin Lake has nice cutts, some of which could break a line. On the way back out, make the side trip to Sliderock Lake for some of the healthiest brook trout anywhere in the Beartooths. Pack them in snow while you finish fishing, and then take them home for dinner.

TRAILHEAD 9
ISLAND LAKE

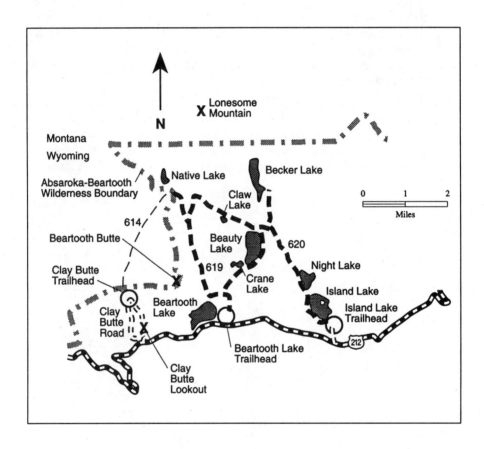

Montana

Wyoming

X Lonesome Mountain

N

Absaroka-Beartooth Wilderness Boundary

Native Lake

Becker Lake

Claw Lake

614

Beauty Lake

620

Beartooth Butte

Clay Butte Trailhead

619

Night Lake

Crane Lake

Island Lake

Beartooth Lake

Island Lake Trailhead

Clay Butte Road

Clay Butte Lookout

Beartooth Lake Trailhead

212

0   1   2
Miles

OVERVIEW

This trailhead is officially named "Island Lake Trailhead," but perhaps a more appropriate name would be "Top of the World Trailhead." Looking around at the surrounding high country, it sure seems like the top of the world. In fact, the Top of the World Store is only 1 mile to the west. The trails start at 9,518 feet, and obviously, they can't climb too much from that point. Therefore, all trips starting from this trailhead are made-to-order for people who don't like big hills.

The trailhead is right in the middle of the uniquely beautiful Wyoming high lakes country. It's hard to believe that this isn't officially part of the Absaroka-Beartooth Wilderness, but it's just as wild and the Forest Service manages it "to preserve its wilderness character." Backcountry travelers don't officially cross the wilderness boundary until they reach the Montana-Wyoming state line.

Dozens of lakes are found within a short walk of the trailhead. Even the trailhead itself is on the shores of magnificent Island Lake. The campground here is popular and usually full. Come during mid-week and early in the day for a chance to land a site here. Even the trailhead parking lot sometimes fills to capacity.

This trailhead is more suited to families and beginners than any trailhead in the Beartooths. The scenery is outstanding, yet exploring requires little effort. But keep in mind that these trails run at or above timberline in an alpine environment. The weather can change quickly and severely, so be watchful and prepared.

Experienced, ambitious hikers can also enjoy a number of trips from this trailhead. Perhaps more than any other trailhead, hikers can simply pull out a topo map and decide where to go, paying little attention to the trails. Many people set up a base camp at some fairly accessible lake and then spend several days taking forays to new places that look interesting on the map. This is a great place to practice and become proficient at off-trail travel and using a compass and topo map.

The trails originate in Wyoming, and at some point, may enter Montana. Those planning to fish here need to know where one state ends and the other begins. To fish in both states, obtain fishing licenses and regulations for both states.

Much of this area is easily accessible to horses, and as a result, many of the lakes were planted with brook trout in the first half of the century. The rationale was that brookies are hearty, easily reproduce, and could establish reproducing populations—which they did. Today, brookies provide excellent fishing for great numbers of aggressive, hungry trout. However, brookies tend to overpopulate these lakes, resulting in smaller fish. On the positive side, 8- to 9-inch brookies may be the tastiest trout of the Beartooths.

Lake trout have been stocked in several lakes with brook trout populations. The lake trout are very predatory, eating brookies, and reducing the population. The result should be larger brookies and better fishing.

FINDING THE TRAILHEAD

The trailhead is easy to find. It's well-marked and located at the end of the access road to Island Lake Campground on the west side of Beartooth Pass. From Cooke City, drive about 25 miles east on U.S. Highway 212 and watch for the turn off on the right. From Red Lodge, it's about a 38-mile drive.

29 *BECKER LAKE*

General description: An easy day hike, overnighter, or accessible base camp.
Total distance: 7.5 miles.
Difficulty: Easy.
Special attractions: A remarkable number of lakes in such a short trip.
Topo maps: USGS—Beartooth Butte; RMS—Wyoming Beartooths.

Key points:

1.0	Night Lake.
2.5	Flake Lake.
2.7	Turn off Wyoming High Lakes Trail 620.
3.3	Mutt and Jeff lakes.
3.6	Becker Lake.

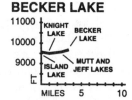

The trail: This is not only a great day hike, but also a perfect choice for that first overnight camping experience with family or children. The trail gains only 175 feet in elevation over 3.5 miles, but just because it's flat doesn't mean it's lacking in scenery. To the contrary, this is one of the most scenic routes in the Beartooths.

From the trailhead the trail closely follows the west shore of Island Lake for most of the first mile. Then it leads less than 0.25 mile over to Night Lake and once again follows the west shore. Small children love this section of trail, but they tend to go slow because there are so many discoveries for them to make.

Continue on, past Flake Lake, also to the east, until you leave Trail 620 and head straight north toward Becker Lake. Be alert not to miss the trail heading to Becker Lake. The way to Becker Lake is not an official Forest Service trail, nor does it show up on the Forest Service or USGS maps.

The trail turns off in a wet meadow just after you leave Flake Lake behind and the Trail 620 turns to the west. The first 50 feet or so is overgrown and hard to see. Then it becomes an excellent trail, almost as well-used as Trail 620. If you miss the trail, simply head off cross-country along the continuous lake between Flake Lake and Jeff Lake. Stay on the west side of the lakes and you'll soon see the trail.

Campsites can be found at Jeff Lake, off to the right just as you first see Jeff Lake. However, most people prefer to go on to Becker Lake.

Go between Mutt Lake and Jeff Lake, crossing over a small stream between the lakes. The two lakes are essentially one lake since the elevation drop between them is about 5 inches. Just past Mutt and Jeff, navigate through a small boulder field. The trail disappears here, so look ahead to where it is clearly defined.

After climbing a small hill (the only one on this trip), hikers are treated with their

Taking a break at Night Lake during an easy day hike.

first view of Becker Lake, with incredibly sheer cliffs on the west bank and 11,409-foot Lonesome Mountain dominating the northern horizon. Leave the trail here, and head off along the south shore of the lake to several campsites just right for one or two tents. There are no sites suitable for large parties. A base camp here offers plenty of choices for day trips, all of them off trail.

> ➤ **Fishing information:** This route has become very popular with anglers, in part because there is very little elevation gain to fight along the way. As noted earlier, the fishing here tends to lean toward brook trout, a good fish for youngsters learning to fish as well as oldsters looking for lots of action. Keep in mind that brook trout are often easier to catch on hardware than hackle. Island and Night lakes have been stocked with rainbows, but now these two lakes are primarily brook trout fisheries. Becker Lake may hold some cutthroats that have migrated down from Albino Lake.
>
> For some variety and a chance to hook cutthroat trout, head up over the saddle at the end of Becker Lake into Montana and Albino Lake. It is stocked on a four-year basis and has some natural reproduction as well to provide some variation in size.
>
> Golden and Jasper lakes, just over the hill from Albino, harbor slightly larger cutts. Heading west cross-country, anglers can try the Cloverleaf Lakes, sporting some of the best cutthroat fishing in the Beartooths.

General description: A truly spectacular trail, best suited for long day trips.
Total distance: 8.5 miles.
Difficulty: Moderate.
Special attractions: Perhaps the best opportunity to travel through the unique high lake country.
Topo maps: USGS—Beartooth Butte; RMS—Wyoming Beartooths.

Key points:

1.0 Night Lake.
2.5 Flake Lake.
3.2 Junction with Trail 621 to Beartooth Lake Trailhead.
3.3 Beauty Lake.
4.5 Claw Lake.
4.9 Shallow Lake.
5.1 Marmot Lake.
5.3 Horseshoe Lake.
5.8 Junction with Trail 619 to Beartooth Lake Trailhead.
8.5 Beartooth Lake Trailhead.

BEARTOOTH HIGH LAKES

				JUNCTION WITH	
11000		CLAW LAKE	BEARTOOTH BUTTE TRAIL		
10000					BEARTOOTH LAKE
9000		JUNCTION			
8000		WITH BEAUTY	HORSESHOE LAKE		
FT		LAKE TRAIL			
	MILES	5		10	15

Hiking the Beartooth High Lakes Trail.

The trail: This is one of those shuttle trails that requires arranging transportation in advance. Leave a vehicle at the Beartooth Lake Trailhead or arrange with another party to start at Beartooth Lake and meet at Claw Lake or Beauty Lake for lunch so you can trade keys.

Although relatively long, this trail is best suited for a day trip. But plan on taking the entire day to cover the distance, leaving plenty of time to enjoy the scenery. Carry a water filter to save weight rather than packing in several full water bottles; the route follows streams and lakes virtually every step of the way.

The first section of this trail goes along Island, Night, and Flake lakes, as described in the Becker Lake trip. It's flat and scenic, and it stays that way for the rest of the trip.

The trail turns west just after Flake Lake and soon drops down into Beauty Lake, where the scenery matches the name. Just before the lake, look for Trail 621 heading off to the south along the east shore of Beauty Lake. This route offers a shorter hike for those so inclined, but it also misses some great vistas by cutting the trip short.

After a short climb out of the Beauty Lake Basin, continue through an open, alpine plateau to Claw Lake. For an overnight stay, this lake or Grayling Lake (just to the south) probably offer the best choices for campsites. Wood is scarce, so please do without campfires here.

After passing Claw Lake and laboring up another small hill, follow a string of lakes (Shallow, Marmot, Horseshoe, and others). This stretch of trail embodies the essence of the Beartooth High Lakes country—water in every direction with Lonesome Mountain dominating the northern horizon and Beartooth Butte on the western horizon. It really doesn't get much better than this, especially on such an accessible trail.

After Horseshoe Lake, the trail turns south toward Beartooth Lake. For about 0.25 mile, the trail fades away, but it's marked by clearly visible cairns. At the well-marked junction with Trail 619, turn left (south) and continue 2.7 miles in the shadow of Beartooth Butte to the Beartooth Lake Trailhead on US 212.

If this isn't a long enough hike, consider the option of leaving a vehicle at the Clay Butte Trailhead and adding about 3 miles to the trip. For this option, turn right at the junction with Trail 619 and head north around the north side of Beartooth Butte.

This option includes another (and longer) section where the trail fades away to nothing more than cairns, but once you hit Trail 614 to Clay Butte, the trail is well-defined. On the way to Clay Butte, the trail passes through a huge meadow that is one of the best places in the Beartooths for wildflower enthusiasts. The downside of taking the Clay Butte option is a tough, 2-mile climb up to the trailhead from the meadow.

➤ | **Fishing information:** Fishing along this trail leans toward brook trout, although several other species have been planted over the brook trout populations. Fishing is usually excellent in lakes with brookies, but some days even these fish are hard to catch—and sometimes hardware users will outfish the fly fishermen.

Beauty Lake has had cutts stocked over the brookies. Claw, Horseshoe, and Beartooth lakes have all had lake trout planted to feed on the brookies to control their population. Beartooth Lake has had several other species introduced, including rainbows, cutts, goldens, and grayling.

TRAILHEAD 10
BEARTOOTH LAKE

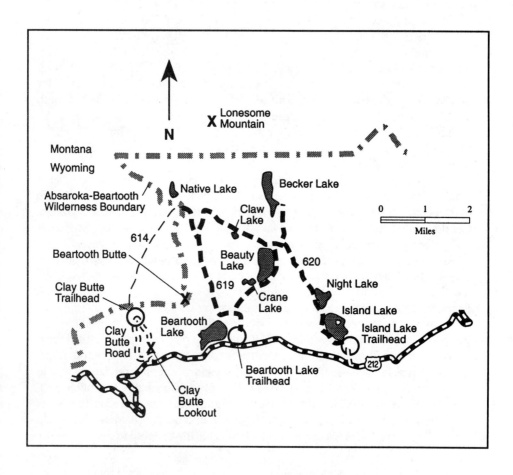

N

X Lonesome
Mountain

Montana
Wyoming

Becker Lake

Native Lake

Absaroka-Beartooth
Wilderness Boundary

Claw
Lake

0   1   2
Miles

614

Beartooth Butte

Beauty
Lake

620

Night Lake

Clay Butte
Trailhead

619

Crane
Lake

Island Lake

Beartooth
Lake

Island Lake
Trailhead

Clay
Butte
Road

212

Beartooth Lake
Trailhead

Clay
Butte
Lookout

OVERVIEW

As at Island Lake, the Beartooth Lake trailhead sits on the edge of a large mountain lake, and the trails start right at the Beartooth Lake Campground. Hikers can camp right at the trailhead and get an early start on the first day—if they are fortunate enough to find a campsite in the popular campground.

Beartooth Lake lies in the shadow of famous 10,514-foot Beartooth Butte, which dominates the western horizon. Beartooth Butte is an enigma, a tiny island of sedimentary rock in a sea of granite making up the Beartooth Mountains. Geologists aren't completely sure how this happened, but they do know that Beartooth Butte contains fossils of some the oldest known plants ever found in North America.

Unlike Island Lake, however, the Beartooth Lake Trailhead parking area is small and at the end of a rough road. Also, the trails leave the trailhead in a slightly confusing manner, so read the directions for each hike carefully to make sure you're on the right one.

This trailhead is in Wyoming. Those planning to fish need to know where one state ends and the other begins. To fish in both states, carry licenses and regulations for both states.

FINDING THE TRAILHEAD

From Cooke City, drive east about 23 miles on U.S. Highway 212 to a well-marked turnoff for Beartooth Lake Campground. From Red Lodge it's about 40 miles west of Red Lodge—and about 1 mile west of the Top of the World Store. Once in the campground, it might take a few minutes to find the trailhead. The likely looking

Beautiful Beartooth Butte. Michael S. Sample photo.

spot on the left just past the entrance is actually a picnic area and boat launch. The trailhead is at the north end of the campground.

But it might be best to park in the lot at the picnic area near the entrance to the campground. The last 100 yards to the trailhead is rough, and the parking area right at the trailhead is small and not well-suited for passenger cars.

CROSS REFERENCE

Refer to the "Beartooth High Lakes" trail starting at the Island Lake Trailhead. This trip could easily be done in reverse, starting at the Beartooth Lake Trailhead.

THE TRAILS

> Beauty Lake
> Claw Lake Loop
> Native Lake Base Camp

31 BEAUTY LAKE

General description: A nice day hike suitable for children.
Total distance: 3.2 miles.
Difficulty: Easy.
Special attractions: A good choice for families.
Topo maps: USGS—Beartooth Butte; RMS—Wyoming Beartooths.

Key points:

0.2	Junction with trail to Beauty Lake.
1.4	Junction with trail to Crane Lake.
1.6	South edge of Beauty Lake.
2.4	Junction with Beartooth High Lakes Trail 620.

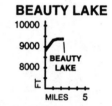

The trail: This trail leaves from a major vehicle campground and is one of the most accessible trails in the Beartooths. Consequently, the trail to Beauty Lake receives heavy use—compared to most other trails in the Beartooths, but not heavy compared to short day hikes in most national parks.

Right at the trailhead the trail is faint. After crossing Beartooth Creek, however, the trail becomes well defined and stays that way all the way to Beauty Lake. In less than 0.25 mile the trail splits. Trail 619 veers off to the left toward Beartooth Butte. Go right on Trail 621 to Beauty Lake.

A gradual climb of about 500 feet leads through lush forest with lots of wildflowers and mushrooms. The trail is rocky in a few places, but is still nicely suited for families with small children. It's rare for such great scenery to grace such a short hike. And it's all downhill on the way back to the trailhead.

Checking out Beauty Lake.

After 1.4 miles, look for Crane Lake off to the left (west) and a trail splitting off in that direction. Those looking for a place to stay overnight will find better campsites along the south shore of Crane Lake than at Beauty Lake.

To get to Beauty Lake, take the right fork in the trail and continue north for less than 0.25 mile. Undoubtedly, visitors here will all agree that this lake lives up to its name. This large, clear, alpine lake boasts several sandy beaches just right for wading on a warm day.

Most people consider Beauty Lake a leisurely day trip. Others hurry by on their way to some more remote spot. But it's also a nice spot to camp. If you do, however, please resist the temptation to build a campfire.

➤ **Fishing information:** Beartooth Lake has been stocked with lake trout, which have thinned the brook trout population. The remaining brookies are larger than average size. Beartooth Lake has had several introductions of other species including rainbows, cutts, goldens, and grayling.

Even though other species have been planted in Beauty Lake, the fishing is still dominated by brook trout. Crane Lake has had cutts stocked over the brookies. Fishing in both lakes is excellent.

32 CLAW LAKE LOOP

General description: A moderate day hike or easy overnighter, a good choice for that first backpacking trip.

Total distance: 8.3 miles.

Difficulty: Moderate.

Special attractions: A rare, short loop returning to the same trailhead.

Topo maps: USGS—Beartooth Butte. RMS—Wyoming Beartooths.

Key points:

0.2	Junction with Trail 621 to Beauty lake. Bear left.
2.9	Junction with Beartooth High Lakes Trail 620.
3.9	Horseshoe Lake.
4.1	Marmot Lake.
4.3	Shallow Lake.
4.7	Claw Lake.
5.9	Junction with Trail 621. Bear right.
6.7	South end of Beauty Lake.
6.9	Crane Lake.
8.3	Beartooth Lake Trailhead.

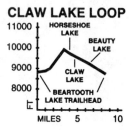

CLAW LAKE LOOP

Stopping to take in the scenery above Horseshoe Lake.

The trail: This trip works either clockwise or counter-clockwise, but clockwise seems slightly easier. This is one of the rare opportunities to trace a short loop returning to the same trailhead; most trips of this length are shuttle or out-and-back trails.

Perhaps the most troublesome spot on the entire trip is the stream crossing right at the trailhead. Earlier in the season, in June and July, this stream carries lots of water, so be careful. Even though children might have some difficulty crossing this stream, the rest of the trip is quite safe. There are five more stream crossings, but none of them are hazardous, and it's usually possible to cross on rocks and keep your feet dry.

Less than 0.25 mile from the trailhead, watch for the junction with Trail 621 to Beauty Lake. To do this trip clockwise, turn left to stay on Trail 619 and head for Beartooth Butte. The return route of this loop comes down Trail 621 to this junction on the final leg to the trailhead.

The first part of the trail hugs the north shoreline of beautiful Beartooth Lake. Some parts of the trail can get quite marshy, especially in June and July. Then, after crossing Beartooth Creek, the trail turns north through the shadow of spectacular Beartooth Butte for another 2 miles to the junction with Beartooth High Lakes Trail 620.

Turn right onto the Beartooth High Lakes Trail and don't be surprised when the trail fades away for about 0.25 mile. A series of cairns clearly marks the way. At the top of a small ridge (the highest point on this trail, about 9,900 feet), the trail becomes well defined again. From this point onto Claw Lake, the trail skirts the south edge of a chain of lakes. Beyond the lakes to the north looms awesome, 11,409-foot Lonesome Mountain.

Continue 1 mile down the trail to Claw Lake. This is the best place for an overnight camp on this loop. There are several excellent campsites on the southwestern shore of Claw Lake, some suitable for large parties. Downed wood is scarce here so please refrain from lighting a campfire. For more privacy, move out of sight of the trail by going a few more hundred yards south to Grayling Lake. The trek around sprawling Grayling Lake makes a scenic side trip.

From Claw Lake, it's slightly more than 1 mile to the junction with Trail 621, which heads south along the east shore of Beauty Lake and past Crane Lake back to the Beartooth Lake Trailhead. Drop your pack at this junction and walk over to the rocky ledge on the north end of Beauty Lake for a fantastic view of the well-named lake. This is a great place to eat lunch for day hikers on this loop. There are several more views to equal this one farther along the lake's edge.

➤ | **Fishing information:** Claw, Horseshoe, and Beartooth lakes have all been planted with lake trout to act as predators to the brook trout populations. For the most part, the fishing along this route is the standard brook trout fare. Sorry, there aren't any grayling left in Grayling Lake.

33 *NATIVE LAKE BASE CAMP*

General description: An easily accessible base camp.
Total distance: 8 miles, not counting side trips.
Difficulty: Easy.
Special attractions: Incredible number of alpine lakes within a short distance of base camp.
Topo maps: USGS—Beartooth Butte, Muddy Creek, Castle Mountain, and Silver Run Peak; RMS—Wyoming Beartooths and Alpine-Mount Maurice.

Key points:

NATIVE LAKE BASE CAMP

0.2   Junction with Trail 621 to Beauty Lake. Bear left.

2.9   Junction with Beartooth High Lakes Trail 620. Bear left.

3.6   Turn off to Clay Butte Trailhead.

4.0   Native Lake.

The trail: Native Lake is an ideal place for a base camp for those who don't want to carry their big packs very far but still want get into some remote wilderness. How to get there, however, can be a tough decision. Going in at the Beartooth Lake Trailhead is the shortest way. But the Clay Butte and Island Lake trailheads also offer access to this area.

Consider arranging a shuttle at a different trailhead to avoid retracing your steps on the way out. With two vehicles, it's best to leave a vehicle at Beartooth Lake and then go in at the Clay Butte Trailhead. Then the entire trip is downhill, with the exception of a minor hill just before Native Lake. The start at Clay Butte is at 9,600 feet, and the end at Beartooth Lake is at 8,900.

Regardless of which trailhead you use, the way into Native Lake can be nearly effortless compared to many trails in the Beartooths. All three trails go through gorgeous, open, alpine country, dotted with lakes and carpeted with wildflowers.

From Beartooth Lake Trailhead, head north on Trail 619. There are two trails that leave the trailhead, so be careful not to get on Trail 621 to Beauty Lake. If you do, the punishment will be 2 extra miles of famous Beartooth High Lakes country before reaching Native Lake.

Start out hiking around the north edge of Beartooth Lake on the edge of some moist meadows. Beartooth Butte provides a magnificent backdrop on the western horizon most of the way into Native Lake. The trail crosses Beartooth Creek twice, but it's usually easy to find a way across on rocks without getting your feet wet.

At the junction with Beartooth High Lakes Trail 620, bear left and keep going north on Trail 619. About 0.5 mile after the junction, watch for a trail and a string of cairns going off to the west through the pass on the north side of Beartooth Butte. These cairns lead down to Trail 614 to Clay Butte.

Continue northwest on the main trail another 0.5 mile to Native Lake. The trail is well-defined the entire way.

Camp on the bench above the trail on the west side of the lake. There are several excellent campsites here, and they're spacious enough for large parties. Camp is at 9,500 feet, high above timberline, so even though there is a limited supply of firewood in this area, please don't give in to the temptation to start a fire.

From Native Lake, there are plenty of options for adventurous side trips. Set up camp and start exploring the area. This is a great place to practice using a compass and topo map.

> **Fishing information:** Native Lake is a cutthroat exception to the brook trout theme found throughout this area. If the cutts are being stubborn, many of the lakes in the area sport voracious populations of brookies. The nearby Beartooth High Lakes Trail provides access to many of these, with lake trout having been added to both T and Lamb lakes.
>
> The Montana state line is about 1 mile north of Native Lake, so anglers must make sure they have the proper state license(s). North of Lonesome Lake, heading cross-country, are Golden and Jasper lakes, both offering some nice cutthroat trout fishing. Just to the west is the Cloverleaf chain of lakes, with a great cutthroat fishery.

WHERE TO GO FROM NATIVE LAKE

The Beartooth High Lake area provides abundant opportunities for moderately easy off-trail side trips. Day trips in this area are less advanced than other areas in the Beartooths, and they provide a good chance to get familiar with off-trail travel without getting in over your head. Here's a list of suggestions rated for difficulty as follows: "Human" (easy for almost everyone, including children), "Semi-Human" (moderately difficult) or "Animal" (don't try it unless you're very fit and wilderness-wise). Also refer to more detailed rating information in the chapter, "Using this Guidebook."

Destination	Difficulty
Box Lakes	Human
Surprise Lake	Human
Mule Lake	Human
Thiel Lake	Human
Martin Lake Basin	Human
Hidden Lake	Semi-Human
Swede Lake	Semi-Human
Lonesome Mountain	Animal
Cloverleaf Lakes	Animal
Jasper & Golden Lakes	Animal
T Lake	Semi-Human
Lonesome Lake	Semi-Human
Beartooth Butte	Animal
Claw & Grayling Lakes	Human

TRAILHEAD 11
CLAY BUTTE

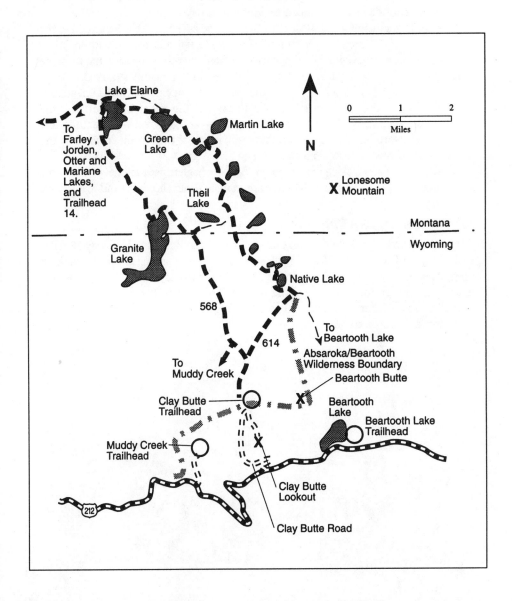

OVERVIEW

Clay Butte is one of those rare trailheads that allows travelers to go downhill instead of up at the beginning of a trip. In fact, the trailhead, at 9,600 feet, is almost the highest point on any trail leaving from it. The Martin Lake and Green Lake trails get up to about 9,800 feet for a short distance, but the rest of the time they run at a lower elevation than the trailhead parking lot.

Clay Butte and neighboring Beartooth Butte to the east and Table Mountain to the south are the only outcrops on the entire Beartooth Plateau still covered with sedimentary rock. Erosion removed the sedimentary rock from the rest of the area, but for some reason, still somewhat unclear to geologists, these three remnants survived.

Most people are in a big hurry to hit the trail when they get to the trailhead, but here it's worth taking an extra 15 minutes to drive to the top of Clay Butte for the view. It's only another mile to the lookout, where—at 9,811 feet—a splendid view is had of the Beartooth Plateau. From this vista, much of the terrain covered by the trails leaving from this trailhead can be seen.

As at other trailheads along the Beartooth Highway, anglers need to know which state they are in, so they can be sure to have the appropriate fishing license(s) and regulations.

FINDING THE TRAILHEAD

The well-marked Clay Butte Road 142 turns north off the Beartooth Highway 20 miles east of Cooke City or 43 miles west of Red Lodge. Any passenger car can make it up the moderately steep, well-maintained gravel road to Clay Butte Lookout, but it's not recommended for vehicles pulling trailers. The road to the trailhead turns off to the left about 1.5 miles from the Beartooth Highway. Parking is limited, with no room for large horse trailers.

The Yellowstone Institute "Backpacking the Beartooths" class at the Clay Butte Trailhead.

Hiking through the large, flower-filled meadow after leaving the Clay Butte trailhead.
Michael S. Sample photo.

THE TRAILS

Upper Granite Lake
Martin Lake Base Camp
Green Lake Loop
Jorden Lake

34 *UPPER GRANITE LAKE*

General description: An out-and-back trip on a well-used trail suitable for a long day trip or an overnighter.
Total distance: 10.4 miles.
Difficulty: Moderate.
Special attractions: One of the largest, deepest, most majestic mountain lakes in the Beartooths.
Topo maps: USGS—Muddy Creek and Castle Mountain; RMS—Wyoming Beartooths and Alpine-Mount Maurice.

Key points:

- 1.2 Junction with Trail 614 to Native Lake.
- 1.7 Junction with Trail 618 to Muddy Creek.
- 4.1 Junction with trail to Thiel Lake.
- 5.2 Upper Granite Lake.

UPPER GRANITE LAKE

10000
GRANITE LAKE
9000
JUNCTION WITH TRAIL 614
8000

ft.

MILES 5

The trail: This is the typical hike in the mountains, only in reverse. It's downhill all the way to the lake and uphill all the way out. Because the trail to Upper Granite Lake stays moist until late in the season, it's not suited for use by backcountry horsemen.

The route is, however, popular with backpackers, and when you get to Granite Lake the reason for this becomes clear. It's hard to believe such a large, beautiful lake so close to a paved highway doesn't have a road to it, vehicle campgrounds, cabins lining the shoreline, and motorboats pulling water skiers. Instead, visitors find a pristine, forested lake straddling the Montana-Wyoming border, protected on all sides by the Absaroka-Beartooth Wilderness.

The first 2 miles of the trail go through open meadows rich in wildflowers, especially early in the season. For wildflower buffs, this is one of the best trails in the Beartooths. And if you ever grow weary of wildflowers, look up. In every direction, on every horizon, the rich greens of the high mountain meadows rise to a panorama of snow-capped peaks. Lonesome Mountain looms to the northeast and Pilot and Index peaks mark the western view.

This trail has some wet sections, and it can get churned up by horses to make travel difficult for hikers. Later in the season, however, the boggy areas dry up and make travel easy.

Upper Granite Lake has several campsites. There's plenty of wood for a campfire.

Upper Granite Lake.

> **Fishing information:** Granite Lake straddles the Wyoming–Montana border, but there is no official agreement between the states on this joint jurisdiction. Technically, anglers should be careful to fish only in the state for which they carry a license. Perhaps the safest approach is to carry licenses from both states.
>
> Granite Lake supports brook trout, rainbows, and cutthroats. There is also talk of planting lake trout. Brook trout dominate the fishery, but there are plenty of other fish. The Montana Department of Fish, Wildlife and Parks also stocks grayling, when available, in Spaghetti and Skeeter lakes.

---

35 *MARTIN LAKE BASE CAMP*

General description:	An excellent base camp trip into one of the most scenic sections of the Beartooths, with many opportunities for side trips.
Total distance:	12.5 miles.
Difficulty:	Moderate.
Special attractions:	Multitudes of scenic, trout-filled lakes, a high-altitude waterfall.
Topo maps:	USGS—Muddy Creek, Beartooth Butte, Castle Mountain, and Silver Run Peak; RMS—Wyoming Beartooths and Alpine-Mount Maurice.

Key points:

1.2 Junction with Trail 568 to Upper Granite Lake.

2.9 Junction with Trail 619 from Beartooth Lake Trailhead.

3.1 Native Lake.

4.2 Mule Lake.

4.7 Thiel Lake.

6.5 Martin Lake Basin.

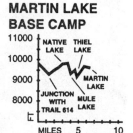

The trail: For those who like to spend one hard day getting into a beautiful base camp and then spend several days doing scenic day trips, this is an ideal choice.

Trail 614 starts out downhill but turns uphill after 1 mile at the junction of Trail 568 to Upper Granite Lake. Turn right and stay on Trail 614. For the first 2.5 miles, the trail travels through an enormous, high-altitude meadow carpeted with wildflowers. At one point, the trail fades away into a string of cairns, so watch carefully for the next trail marker.

About 0.25 mile before Native Lake the trail meets Trail 619 coming from Beartooth Lake. Turn left (west) on Trail 619. Native Lake is the beginning of a long string of lakes. It's tempting to look for campsites along the way, but the best is yet to come at Martin Lake. Be prepared for short, steep climbs just before and after Mule

Spogen Lake and Falls.

Lake and a long, strenuous climb into the Martin Lake Basin that starts just after Thiel Lake. Be careful not to miss Thiel Lake. It's off to the left (south) at the bottom of the hill after Mule Lake, just after the trail breaks out into a lush meadow.

Martin Lake Basin is one of the most fascinating places in the Beartooths. Four major lakes (Martin, Wright, Spogen, and Whitcomb) are linked by a trout-filled stream, and there's a spectacular, high-altitude waterfall between Wright and Spogen lakes. The waterfall seems larger and more majestic here at 9,600-feet.

Overnighters can camp almost anywhere in the basin, especially around Wright and Martin lakes. This is like a five-star hotel; every room with a view, nature's penthouse. Firewood, however, is in short supply and essential to the extraordinary charm of this basin, so resist the temptation to have a campfire.

As is plain from the topo map, this is lake country. Dozens of lakes lie within a day's trek from this basin. Even avid explorers could spend a week here and not see the same lake twice. Don't forget to spend one of those days simply hiking around the four lakes in the basin to fully appreciate a place that would put most national parks to shame.

Another factor making this a better base camp than most is that hikers don't have to retrace the exact same route on the way out. On the return trip, from the bottom of the big hill to Thiel Lake, leave Trail 619 and follow a well-used trail that traverses the east side of Thiel Lake. This isn't an official Forest Service trail and doesn't show on the topo or national forest maps, but it's well-maintained and signed at the south end. In less than 1 mile it intersects with Trail 568, which goes to Upper Granite Lake. Turn left (south) at this junction and follow this well-used trail back to the trailhead. This still means retracing your steps the last uphill mile to the trailhead from the junction of trails 568 and 614, but most of the trip out will be new country.

Hidden Lake.

Fishing information: Most of the lakes in this area were stocked with brook trout, and the chain of lakes in Martin Lake Basin is named after the men who hauled the brook trout in. The brookies here are average for the Beartooths with Whitcomb Lake and Lake Estelle having slightly larger fish.

For variation, Trail Lake (appropriately named) has cutthroats that are stocked, but which also reproduce. Head upstream from Martin Lake to reach the cutthroat hotbed found in the Cloverleaf Lakes.

Earlier along the route in, a side trip to Swede and Hidden lakes is worthwhile for the cutthroats found there. Goldens were once found in Hidden Lake, and a few may still remain.

WHERE TO GO FROM MARTIN LAKE

The Martin Lake Basin provides abundant opportunities for moderately easy off-trail side trips. Here's a list of suggestions rated for difficulty as follows: "Human" (easy for almost everyone, including children), "Semi-Human" (moderately difficult), or "Animal" (don't try it unless you're very fit and wilderness-wise). Also refer to more detailed rating information in the chapter, "Using this Guidebook."

Destination	Difficulty
Box Lakes	Human
Surprise Lake	Human
Mule Lake	Human
Thiel Lake	Human
Around Martin Lake Basin	Human
Hidden Lake	Semi-Human
Swede Lake	Semi-Human
Cloverleaf Lakes	Animal
Kidney Lake	Human
Marmot Lake	Semi-Human
Trail Lake	Human
Green Lake	Human
Lake Estelle	Semi-Human
Sierra Creek	Semi-Human

General description: A long loop on the southwest edge of the Beartooth Plateau, best suited for at least two nights out, with one short off-trail section. One short section is impassable for horses.

Total distance: 19.4 miles.

Difficulty: Difficult.

Special attractions: A short, easy, off-trail section can be a confidence builder, and unlike some trips, there's plenty of opportunities to get your feet wet.

Topo maps: USGS—Muddy Creek, Beartooth Butte, Castle Mountain, and Silver Run Peak; RMS Wyoming Beartooths and Alpine-Mount Maurice.

Key points:

1.2   Junction with Trail 568 to Upper Granite Lake.

2.9   Junction with Trail 619 from Beartooth Lake Trailhead.

3.1   Native Lake.

4.3   Mule Lake.

4.6   Thiel Lake.

6.5   Martin Lake Basin.

7.8   Green Lake.

8.8   Sierra Creek.

10.1   Upper Lake Elaine and Junction with Trail 568 to Farley Lake.

10.9   Lower Lake Elaine.

13.7   Upper Granite Lake.

14.9   Junction with trail to Thiel Lake.

17.9   Junction with trail to Muddy Creek.

18.2   Junction with Trail 614.

19.4   Clay Butte Trailhead.

GREEN LAKE LOOP

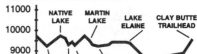

The trail: This trip begins by following the route described earlier in this section for the Martin Lake Base Camp trip. Although the Martin Lake Basin offers the best campsites for the first night out, it's also possible to make camp earlier in the day near one of the lakes along the trail. Native, Box, Mule, and Thiel lakes all boast excellent campsites. Thiel Lake is a frequent overnight stay for backcountry horsemen.

Build a campfire only if necessary; downed wood is scarce here, except perhaps at Thiel and Mule lakes. Be prepared for short, steep climbs just before and after Mule Lake, and be careful to not miss Thiel Lake, about 0.25 mile south of the trail where it opens up into a lush meadow at the bottom of a short hill.

Regardless of where you spend your first night, continue along Trail 619 the next morning. Just after Thiel Lake, start a long, strenuous climb into the Martin Lake

Basin. It's a tough grind, but the reward at the end is well worth it. Martin Lake Basin is one of the most alluring spots in the Beartooths. Four major lakes (Martin, Wright, Spogen, and Whitcomb) stair-step through this magnificent basin, and there's a spectacular, high-altitude waterfall between Wright and Spogen lakes. The waterfall seems larger and more majestic here at 9,600 feet.

There are plenty of campsites in the basin, especially around Wright and Martin lakes. Downed wood is limited here and essential to the aesthetics, so please resist the temptation to have a campfire.

Since this is one of the most spectacular spots in the Beartooths, plan to spend the night in this basin. For those who hiked all the way in on their first day, this area is worth a two-night stay. There are plenty of enticing day trips you can take from Martin Lake Basin. For example, a leisurely hike around the basin can take most of a day. More ambitious explorers can trek up to Cloverleaf Lakes.

The creek between Wright and Spogen lakes must be forded, so when selecting a campsite consider whether you want wet feet that night or first thing the next morning.

After spending a night in the Martin Lake Basin you might have to force yourself to hit the trail the next morning. After a small hill to get out of the basin, the route skirts Trail Lake before heading down a steep hill into the gorgeous Green Lake valley. Going down this grade is all the argument needed against doing this trip in reverse. This hill makes the climb from Thiel Lake to Martin Lake Basin seem mild.

At Green Lake, do not continue around the lake to the south, even though the trail appears to head in that direction. Instead, turn north and cross the inlet stream and head around the north side of Green Lake on a less defined trail. This isn't an official Forest Service trail, nor is it on the national forest map or topo map, but it's an easily followed pathway around the lake to Sierra Creek.

If for some reason you decide not to camp in the Martin Lake Basin, camp instead at the head of Green Lake or after crossing Sierra Creek. These are serviceable campsites but not of the five-star caliber of those in the Martin Lake Basin.

The Sierra Creek ford can be fairly difficult early in the season, so be careful. After the ford, the trail leaves the Green Lake shoreline and heads straight west to Lake Elaine. Again, this isn't an official trail and it is not maintained or marked, but it's still fairly easy to navigate. The trail through this section fades away in several wet meadows. Stay on the south edge of these meadows.

At Lake Elaine, traverse the north shoreline—including a short boulder field—until you hit well-used Trail 568. Be careful in the boulder field—it can be dangerous, especially when carrying a big pack or when the rocks are wet. Turn left (south) on Trail 568, which hugs the west shore of Lake Elaine for about 1 mile.

Shortly after leaving Lake Elaine, the trail heads down a steep hill, another good reason not to do this trip in reverse. This downhill grade receives heavy horse traffic, which has ground up the rock into a fine dust that can make footing precarious, so watch your step. From the bottom of this climb, it's a pleasant 2 miles to upper Granite Lake, a good place to camp.

Granite Lake is a huge mountain lake fed by massive Lake Creek, which splinters into six channels just before tumbling into Granite Lake. Some folks moan and groan about having to cross six streams, but imagine how difficult the crossing would be if Lake Creek stayed in one channel.

The first view of Granite Lake is all the enticement most people need to stay, so why not? Choose from any of the numerous campsites at the upper end of the lake.

From Granite Lake, the trail gradually climbs all the way to the Clay Butte Trailhead. This final stretch can become fairly muddy in frequent boggy sections. The hardest part of the trip, it seems, is the last uphill mile which seemed so pleasant three or four days ago.

Actually, this trip can be done as a shuttle by leaving a vehicle at the Muddy Creek Trailhead. This avoids the uphill grind back to the Clay Butte Trailhead. The trail along the west side of Granite Lake leads out Muddy Creek. Another option is to continue toward Clay Butte, but then turn off on a trail that heads west about 1 mile before the trailhead and drops steeply down to Muddy Creek. If you go around Granite Lake, you must make a difficult ford of Lake Creek as it leaves Granite Lake.

➤ | **Fishing Information:** This route is much the same as that noted for the Martin Lake Base Camp route, so refer to that fishing information. Green Lake contains oodles of pan-sized brookies. Take some of these brook trout with you—those remaining will thank you.

From Green Lake, try a nice side trip up Sierra Creek to Crystal or Flat Rock lakes. The cutthroats stocked here provide a nice contrast to the brook trout found in surrounding lakes. Both Crystal and Flat Rock have eight-year stocking cycles and were last stocked in 1994.

From camp near Lake Creek at Granite Lake, a side trip can be made to Skeeter and Spaghetti lakes for grayling. When grayling are available, DFWP stocks these lakes. It's a tough, off-trail trip that should be attempted only by those proficient in reading a topo map and compass.

37 *JORDEN LAKE*

General description: A long shuttle on the southwest edge of the Beartooth Plateau, best suited for at least three nights out for hikers and one night for backcountry horsemen.

Total distance: 23.9 miles.

Difficulty: Moderate.

Special attractions: A series of large, trout-filled lakes and a variety of scenery. A popular trip for backcountry horsemen.

Topo maps: USGS—Muddy Creek, Castle Mountain, and Fossil Lake; RMS—Wyoming Beartooths, Alpine-Mount Maurice, and Cooke City-Cutoff Mountain.

Key points:

The trail: The first 5.2 miles of this trip are identical to the Upper Granite Lake trip described earlier in this section. Head downhill from the Clay Butte Trailhead, through open mountain parks and forest to Upper Granite Lake. This is a good place to camp the first night

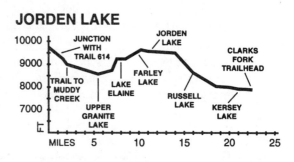

JORDEN LAKE

out, particularly for those who started late in the day. Lake Elaine offers only limited camping, especially for large parties, and it would be a long day with a backpack to get to Farley or Jorden lakes for the first night out.

From Granite Lake, the trail climbs gradually along Lake Creek until just before Lake Elaine. Here it goes madly uphill with poor footing. Heavy horse traffic has pounded this section into dust, making it slippery even when it isn't wet.

At the top of the hill, the forest opens up to beautiful Lake Elaine. Follow the west shore of the lake for about 1 mile until the trail veers off to the left (northwest) at the upper end of the lake. There are two campsite along the west shore.

Shortly after leaving Lake Elaine, climb just enough to break out above timberline. It's about 2 miles to Farley Lake, but it's only another mile to Jorden Lake. Both lakes have plenty of quality campsites and are similar in appearance, with Jorden Lake the larger of the two. Jorden Lake is a popular destination for backcountry horsemen.

At this point, several options are possible. Set up base camp at Farley or Jorden, spending several days visiting lakes in the vicinity (such as a trip to the well-named Desolation Lakes area). Or head back out via Copeland Lake, as outlined in the

Copeland Lake trip. But perhaps the best option, if a shuttle can be arranged, is to ramble over to Trail 567 to the Clarks Fork Trailhead. From Jorden Lake, this route offers a highly enjoyable trek along a continuous string of beautiful lakes in both forested and subalpine environments.

From Jorden Lake follow the trail 1.5 miles northwest to Otter Lake. The trail from Otter to Russell Lake isn't on the national forest or topo maps, but it's well-defined on the ground most of the way. In a few places around Otter and Mariane lakes, the trail fades away, but the route is still easy to follow. After dropping down a steep grade from Mariane Lake to Russell Lake, the route dips below timberline into a fairly moist forested landscape. It then meets "The Beaten Path" (i.e. the main thorough-fare through the Beartooths, Trail 567) about 0.25 mile from Russell Lake. Turn left (south) on Trail 567.

Russell Lake offers a conveniently located campsite for the third night out. Perhaps because of its convenient location, however, Russell Lake is very heavily used. The Forest Service discourages camping here, especially by backcountry horsemen because of the heavy impact stock has had on this area and the limited forage. Hikers can camp at either the upper end or lower end of the lake but may have to cross the stream to reach the best campsites. Hikers can also push on to Fox or Rock Island lakes to camp. Both lakes have a limited number of campsites that are not well-suited for horses. However, there's a good chance that these campsites will be occupied; both Fox and Rock Island are popular overnight camping destinations from the Clarks Fork Trailhead.

Hikers who stay at Russell Lake should start early on the last day. It's a fairly easy 8 miles downhill on the way out. But there are several tempting, short side trips to Fox, Rock Island, Vernon, and Curl lakes. Approaching Kersey Lake, the aftermath of the dramatic fires of 1988 becomes apparent, but the rest of the trip you travel through unburned forest. Also, be sure to watch for where the trail splits into horse and foot paths just after Kersey Lake. Parties with stock go right (west) to a separate trailhead, and parties on foot stay left (east).

➤ | **Fishing information:** Jorden Lake holds a reproducing population of cut-throat trout that adequately complements the scenery. There are two creeks that enter the north side of Jorden Lake, both of which originate at Wid-owed Lake. Starting with Desolation Lake and ending with Widowed Lake, DFWP is trying to establish a reproducing population of golden trout. The trout are there in low numbers, but this experiment can not yet be declared a success.

Many of the lakes along this route contain brook trout, but anglers willing to get off the trail can find other species. Keep in mind, however, that not all lakes contain fish.

Fox Lake sports larger-than-average brookies, nice rainbows, and an occa-sional grayling that works its way down from Cliff Lake.

TRAILHEAD 12
MUDDY CREEK

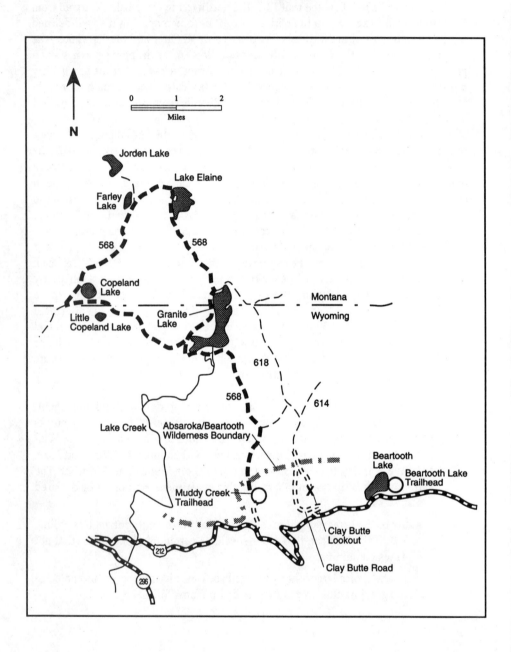

N

0 1 2
Miles

Jorden Lake

Lake Elaine

Farley
Lake

568

568

Copeland
Lake

Montana

Wyoming

Little
Copeland Lake

Granite
Lake

618

568

614

Lake Creek

Absaroka/Beartooth
Wilderness Boundary

Beartooth
Lake

Beartooth Lake
Trailhead

Muddy Creek
Trailhead

X

Clay Butte
Lookout

212

Clay Butte Road

296

OVERVIEW

The Muddy Creek and Copeland Lake area skirts the western flank of the mighty Beartooth Plateau. Most of the area is forested, interspersed with grassy parks. Only the Farley Lake area rises above timberline.

This area has a special, remote charm quite different than much of the Beartooths. It doesn't have as much spectacular mountain scenery as some trails, but as a result, it receives much less use than most of the Beartooths. It is, however, popular with backcountry horsemen.

FINDING THE TRAILHEAD

The trailhead is well-signed on the north side of the Beartooth Highway (U.S. Highway 212), 17.5 miles east of Cooke City or 45.5 west of Red Lodge. It isn't a large trailhead, and parking is limited. The short access road is fairly rough and best suited for high-clearance vehicles.

THE TRAILS

Lower Granite Lake
Copeland Lake Loop

38 *LOWER GRANITE LAKE*

General description: A fairly long, but not strenuous, out-and-back day hike or an easy overnight backpack.
Total distance: 10.4 miles.
Difficulty: Moderate (unless you ford Lake Creek).
Special attractions: A sprawling subalpine lake with good fishing.
Topo maps: USGS—Muddy Creek; RMS—Wyoming Beartooths.

Key points:

0.8   End of jeep road.
2.8   Connecting trail to Clay Butte.
5.2   Lower Granite Lake.

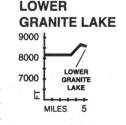

LOWER GRANITE LAKE

The trail: Going up Muddy Creek is the easiest—but the muddiest—way to reach monstrous Granite Lake. Another route to the lower end of Granite Lake is possible from Clay Butte, but the way back to the trailhead will require a near-vertical climb (720 feet elevation gain in 0.8 mile) out of Muddy Creek to connect with Clay Butte Trail 618, plus another 560-foot climb to get to the Clay Butte Trailhead.

The trail starts out from the Muddy Creek Trailhead as a rough jeep road, and vehicles are sometimes parked anywhere along the first 0.8 mile of the trail. Then the trail opens up into an expansive and beautiful meadow. It's also a wet meadow.

The best time to take this hike is late August when the water level in the meadow has dropped. In a few places, the trail can be difficult to find through the tall grass, but the gradient remains almost flat until just before Granite Lake. Here the trail climbs about 200 feet and then drops into the Lake Creek drainage.

The trail arrives at the south end of Granite Lake and turns west to ford the outlet stream, Lake Creek. There are excellent campsites on both sides of the creek here. But beware: fording Lake Creek can be dangerous. A tremendous amount of water leaves Granite Lake, and the flow can be powerful and chest-deep on a short person. This is one of the most hazardous fords in the Beartooths.

➤ | **Fishing information:** Granite Lake supports rainbows and cutthroats, but brook trout dominate the fishery. Fisheries managers are currently discussing the possibility of introducing lake trout to Granite Lake.

39 COPELAND LAKE LOOP

General description: A long loop, just right for a 3- or 4-night backpack.
Total distance: 26.5 miles.
Difficulty: Moderately difficult, with two difficult stream crossings and one steep hill to climb.
Topo maps: USGS—Muddy Creek and Castle Mountain; RMS—Wyoming Beartooths and Alpine-Mount Maurice.

Key points:

COPELAND LAKE LOOP

0.8	End of jeep road.
2.8	Connecting trail to Clay Butte.
5.2	Lower Granite Lake and Lake Creek ford.
6.1	Copeland Lake Trail 612 Junction.
7.7	Upper end of Granite Lake.
7.8	Clay Butte Trail 618 Junction.
10.4	Lower end of Lake Elaine.
11.3	Upper end of Lake Elaine.
12.5	Farley Lake and Junction with trail to Jorden Lake.
16.6	Cooke City Trail 624 Junction.
16.8	Copeland Lake.
17.8	Little Copeland Lake.
20.4	Granite Lake Trail 612 Junction.
21.3	Lower end of Granite Lake, Lake Creek ford.
26.5	Muddy Creek Trailhead.

The trail: The first leg of the hike to the lower end of Granite Lake follows Muddy Creek, well-named for its long series of boggy meadows which are usually muddy early in the summer. The first 0.8 mile is on a seldom-used jeep road.

You will probably want to spend the first night at the lower end of Granite Lake where there are several scenic campsites. It might be tempting to march on for another 2.5 miles to the upper end of Granite Lake, but there are fewer first-class campsites there, and they might be taken. The upper end of the lake gets more use than the lower end. There's also a large horse camp at the upper end.

Rich forests surround aesthetic Granite Lake, and there is ample fuel for buidling a campfire.

Lake Creek leaves Granite Lake at the lower end amid the campsites. Be extra careful fording this stream, especially in the early summer when the water is high. This can be one of the most difficult stream crossings in the Beartooths. Most people have a tough time deciding whether to take the plunge that evening or first thing the next morning.

Shortly after the ford, look for the trail coming in from Copeland Lake on the left. That will be the return leg of this loop. Turn right (north) and follow Trail 568 along the west shore of Granite Lake, one of the largest lakes in the Beartooths and shared by Montana and Wyoming.

At the lake's upper end, Lake Creek splits into six channels before melting into Granite Lake. But you don't have to cross them on this trip.

From here the trip to Lake Elaine starts out easy and mostly flat. But just before Lake Elaine, you are faced with the toughest climb of the trip. Fortunately, it's short. This 0.3-mile climb is not only steep, but dusty and slick. Heavy horse traffic has ground the rock down to a fine sand, creating precarious footing, especially when

Upper Lake Elaine.

wet. Believe it or not, it's easier going up than down this steep slope.

At Lake Elaine, the forest starts to open up, giving great views of another of the largest lakes in the Beartooths. Despite its size, Lake Elaine really doesn't offer much in the way of quality camping, so after soaking in the scenery over lunch, strike west on the trail to Farley Lake for the second night's campsite.

Just before Farley Lake, the trail meets the trail going right (north) to Jorden Lake. Turn left to Farley Lake, which has several campsites but not enough wood for a campfire. Those with energy to spare and who don't mind getting off the trail can go another mile to the more secluded Hipshot or Wade lakes. It's a short cross-country trip to these lakes, so check the topo map carefully before heading off to Wade or Hipshot. Both lakes are about 0.5 mile south of Farley Lake—Wade Lake to the east of the trail and Hipshot to the west.

From Farley Lake the trail heads south, and just before Copeland Lake it meets a trail on the right coming in from the Crazy Creek trailhead. Turn left and continue 0.5 mile to Copeland Lake, which is nestled in a forested pocket with lots of wood for campfires—and a few more mosquitoes than any lake deserves. There's also a large outfitter camp here (with a special use permit from the Forest Service), so at times Copeland Lake could be crowded. Camp at Copeland for the third night, and leave the 9.7-mile trek out to the Muddy Creek trailhead for the final day. The grade is easy down to Granite Lake and the Lake Creek ford. Then there is one short climb out of the basin and into the Muddy Creek drainage.

To do this loop in three days requires at least one double-digit mileage day on the trail unless you risk finding space to camp the first night at the upper end of Granite Lake. From here it's just over 9 miles to Copeland Lake for the second night's stay, leaving 9.7 miles for the last day out.

➤ | **Fishing Information:** Most lakes along this route, including Lake Elaine, contain brook trout. However, Hipshot Lake contains stocked cutthroat trout, and Jorden Lake has natural cutts. Farley Lake provides the best brook trout eatery, with the fish being an inch or so larger than nearby lakes.

TRAILHEAD 13
CRAZY CREEK

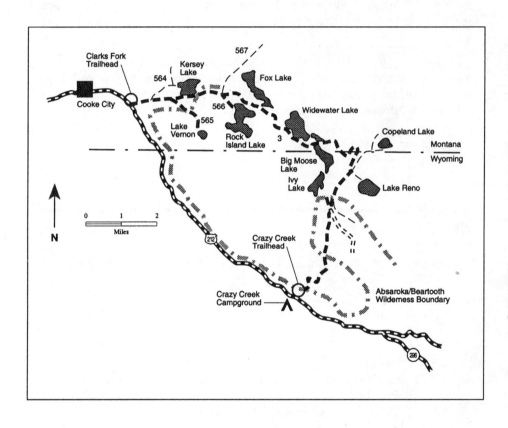

Crazy Creek is the trailhead that everybody drives by on their way to more popular trails that leave from the Cooke City, Beartooth Lake, or Island Lake trailheads. All those who drive by are missing something.

The Crazy Lakes area is drier and more forested than the high-altitude areas, but it's just as wild and beautiful. And it definitely receives much less use than the more popular trails.

The centerpiece of the area, Crazy Creek Falls, is only a short walk from the trailhead. Even if you don't take a longer foray up Crazy Creek, do stop for a few minutes to savor the raw beauty of Crazy Creek Falls.

Some sections of the first part of the Crazy Creek Trail are not within the Absaroka-Beartooth Wilderness. However, with the exception of one jeep road that comes in from the Lily Lake area, the drainage has all the wildness of any wilderness area.

FINDING THE TRAILHEAD

The Crazy Lake Trailhead is 10.7 miles east of Cooke City on the Beartooth Highway (U.S. Highway 212). The trailhead is a turnoff on the north side of the highway across from the Crazy Creek Campground.

THE TRAILS

>Ivy Lake
>Crazy Lakes

40 IVY LAKE

General description:	A moderately long day hike or easy overnighter.
Total distance:	9 miles.
Difficulty:	Moderate.
Topo maps:	USGS—Jim Smith Peak; RMS—Wyoming Beartooths.

Key points:

3.5	Little Moose Lake.
3.7	Junction with jeep road coming in from Lily Lake Area.
4.0	Turn off jeep road onto trail to Ivy Lake.
4.5	Ivy Lake.

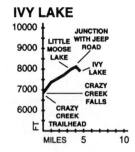

The trail: The Ivy Lake trail starts off with a bang. The first 0.25 mile is paralleled by cascading Crazy Creek Falls. You'll want to stop and marvel at it two or three times along the way.

Much of this trail goes through a drier, sagebrush-type environment with Pilot and Index peaks highlighting the western horizon. Plan to hike this route in early morning or evening to avoid the heat—and for a better chance of seeing those elk and moose that have been sleeping during the hot midday. Just after the trail breaks out of the forest there's one confusing spot. A good (but unofficial) trail juts off to the right. Bear left and head uphill.

About halfway to Ivy Lake the trail wanders through a big wet meadow. Earlier in the season (June and July), it can be difficult to cross this high-altitude marsh without getting your feet wet.

At the 3.5-mile mark, look to the left, down the hill to Little Moose Lake. For a short side trip, drop down and note the unusual "floating shoreline" here.

Less than 0.25 mile after Little Moose Lake, the trail meets a jeep road coming from the Lily Lake area to the east. Continue north along the jeep road for another 0.25 mile before the trail veers off to the left down to Ivy Lake.

There are campsites on the left and right just before the lake. Since this area was partly burned during the 1988 fires, there's plenty of wood for a campfire.

> | **Fishing information:** Ivy Lake is the lowest of a chain of lakes on Crazy Creek. This chain of lakes harbors both brook trout and rainbow trout, and the variety provides for some nice (though not exceptional) fishing. The rainbows are much harder to catch than brookies.

Little Moose Lake is stocked occasionally with cutthroat trout. The weedy nature of the lake makes it a good home for food organisms, so fish may grow large here as they get older.

41 *CRAZY LAKES*

General description: A two- or three-night, late summer shuttle trip.
Total distance: 15.2 miles.
Difficulty: Moderate.
Special attractions: Large beautiful, forested lakes.
Topo maps: USGS—Jim Smith Peak and Fossil Lake; RMS—Wyoming Beartooths and Cooke City-Cutofff Mountain.

Key points:

3.5   Little Moose Lake.
3.7   Junction with jeep road coming in from Lily Lake Area.
3.8   Turn off on Crazy Lakes Trail 612.
5.6   Junction with Trail 3 and Trail 622 to Lake Reno.
7.8   Big Moose Lake.
11.7 Junction with Trail 587.
11.9 Junction with Trail 566 to Rock Island Lake.
12.9 Kersey Lake.
13.7 Junction with Trail 565 to Lake Vernon.
15.2 Clarks Fork Trailhead.

CRAZY LAKES

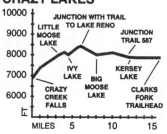

Fishing at Big Moose Lake, one of the Crazy Lakes.

The trail: The first order of business is leaving a vehicle at the Clarks Fork Trailhead. Keep in mind that the Clarks Fork Trailhead is split into two trailheads, one for backpackers and one for backcountry horsemen, so make sure to leave your vehicle at the right one. If you are trading keys with another party, plan on joining up at approximately the halfway point on the west shore of Big Moose Lake.

As described in the Ivy Lake trip, the first 4 miles of the trail start out in a grand manner with Crazy Creek Falls and then go through sagebrush and open forest, with a marsh or two, until meeting the jeep road coming in from the Lily Lake area. At this point, it's easy to get off track.

At the junction where the jeep road heads off to the east, continue north on the jeep road for about 100 yards. At that point a trail angles off the road at about 2 o'clock. Take this trail, even though it isn't marked. If you stay on the road, you'll end up at Ivy Lake.

Actually, if you're out for two nights, make a note of this junction and continue on up the road to Ivy Lake, a good spot for the first night out. Come back to this confusing intersection the next morning. There are several places to camp at Ivy Lake; the best site is on the left just before the lake.

The second choice for the first night out would be Big Moose Lake. You get there by continuing on Trail 612 to the junction with Trail 3 and Trail 622 to Lake Reno. This is a very confusing intersection, so allow an extra half hour to slowly find your way.

Turn left on Trail 3, which angles off at about 10 o'clock about 200 yards before the junction for Lake Reno. Shortly thereafter, the trail seems to abruptly end, but instead, it goes off to the right at about 1 o'clock. It's another 2 miles to Big Moose Lake. If there's time for a side trip, it's only 0.5 mile over to Lake Reno. Camping at Lake Reno is limited and the area tends to be marshy.

At Big Moose Lake it becomes clear why this trip isn't recommended for early in the season, even though the snow burns off of this lower elevation area earlier than most of the Beartooths. Big Moose Lake is, more or less, a big, wide, shallow section of Crazy Creek. To continue the trek, hikers must, in essence, ford Big Moose Lake. In June, this turns into an exhilarating experience, to say the least. In August, it's not too bad. But even in August, don't ford Big Moose Lake where the trail meets the shoreline. It's better to go slightly north where the water has some more current.

The best campsite is on the west side of Big Moose Lake, just north of the trail. There's room for a large party or several parties without anybody losing much privacy. Remember that Forest Service regulations limit the size of parties with stock animals.

Another good choice for the second night out is Rock Island Lake. From Big Moose Lake, it's almost 4 miles to the junction with Trail 567. Turn left (south) here and go about 200 yards to the junction with Trail 566 to Rock Island Lake. Camping is somewhat limited at Rock Island, but once you find a spot big enough for a tent, you'll relish your stay at this gorgeous, productive, deep, forested lake that seems to sprawl everywhere. Set aside several hours of free time if you want to walk around this lake.

From Big Moose Lake the trail is in excellent shape and easy to follow. From Rock Island Lake it's a leisurely 3 miles out to the Clarks Fork Trailhead.

➤ **Fishing information:** The Crazy Lakes are a chain of lakes starting with Fox and Widewater lakes in Montana, Moose Lake straddling the border, and Ivy Lake in Wyoming. The chain of lakes has both brook and rainbow trout and a few grayling. The streams between the lakes sport the same type of fish, and they are easier to locate.

Fox Lake has some above-average brookies and some nice rainbows. Rock Island has a nice mix of cutts and brookies, but many people know this, and anglers can count on some competition, as it is an easy day hike from the Clarks Fork Trailhead to Rock Island Lake.

TRAILHEAD 14

CLARKS FORK OF THE YELLOWSTONE

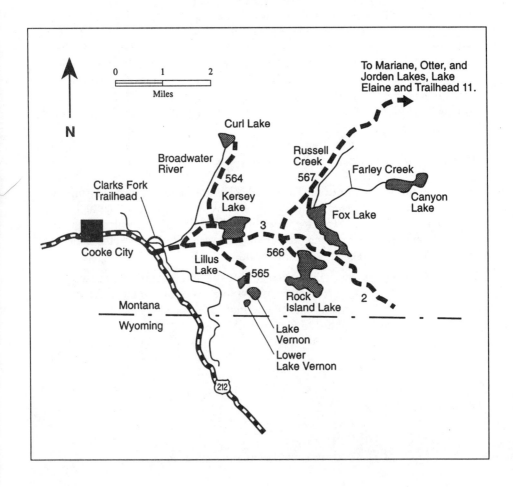

OVERVIEW

Anyone who has been to the Clarks Fork Trailhead could mount a strong argument that it's the most beautiful trailhead in the Beartooths. It rests on the south shoreline of the Clarks Fork of the Yellowstone as the river leaves the Beartooths right at a spectacular falls and large pool, perfect for a dip after a long, hot week in the wilderness. The large grassy area with picnic tables is especially nice for people wanting a leisurely picnic in a gorgeous setting followed by a short day hike. In fact, a worthwhile attraction lies just beyond the trailhead, where a major foot bridge spans the Clarks Fork where it has cut a narrow gorge.

Since this trailhead is the south end of The Beaten Path through the Beartooths, it's obviously heavily used. It's also large, with toilet facilities and plenty of room to park or turn around any vehicle. Visitors might find twenty vehicles parked here, possibly from twenty different states.

All the trips from this trailhead pass by Kersey Lake. There are cabins with vehicle access to the lake. These are private inholdings; one is a Forest Service rental cabin. Kersey Lake is not within the Absaroka-Beartooth Wilderness.

This is actually two trailheads in one. Backcountry horsemen use a companion trailhead just west of the main trailhead, also with a well-signed turnoff along the Beartooth Highway about 0.25 mile to the west. This is the only trailhead in the Beartooths where the Forest Service has provided separate facilities for backcountry horseman and hikers. In addition, the first mile of the trail is also split—the east path is for hikers and the west for horsemen.

Also check out the watchable wildlife interpretive display put up by the Forest Service. It's located on the Beartooth Highway between the entrances to the two trailheads.

The sturdy bridge over the Clarks Fork just down the trail from the Clarks Fork Trailhead.

FINDING THE TRAILHEAD

Take U.S. Highway 212 east from Cooke City for 4.2 miles and turn left (north) onto Forest Road 306. Drive about 0.5 mile to the trailhead. Trail 3 takes off at the far end of this large trailhead and parking area.

CROSS REFERENCE

Be sure to check "The Beaten Path" trail starting at the East Rosebud Trailhead, the Crazy Lakes trail starting at the Crazy Lakes Trailhead, and the "Jorden Lake" trail starting at the Clay Butte Trailhead. All of these trails could be done in reverse by starting at the Clarks Fork Trailhead.

THE TRAILS

> Curl Lake
> Lake Vernon
> Rock Island Lake
> Fox Lake

42 CURL LAKE

General description:	A seldom-used trail suitable for day trips or an overnight stay.
Total distance:	7 miles.
Difficulty:	Moderate.
Topo maps:	USGS—Fossil Lake; RMS—Cooke City-Cutoff Mountain.

Key points:

0.5   Kersey Lake Jeep Road.
1.1   Junction with Trail 564 to Curl Lake.
2.7   Broadwater Meadow Lakes.

CURL LAKE

The trail: For a moderately short trip into a infrequently visited lake, Curl Lake is a good choice. The lack of use shows on the trail. It's difficult to follow in places, especially just before the lake, and early in the year hikers must skirt their way around several bogs to keep their feet dry. With the exception of the first mile, the trail goes through forests burned by the 1988 fires, including along the entire shoreline of Curl Lake.

The good news is hardly anyone goes into Curl Lake, so you will likely have the trail all to yourself.

To find Curl Lake, take Trail 3 from the Clarks Fork Trailhead. After about 0.5 mile, turn left (northeast) at the well-marked junction with the Kersey Lake Jeep Road. From this point on, it's a moderate uphill grade all the way to Curl Lake. Follow the road for another 0.5 mile and turn left (north) on Trail 564.

Trail 564 passes through partially burnt forest and several wet meadows. Then, off to the left, watch for the Broadwater River rushing down to meet the Clarks Fork. Follow this beautiful cascading stream the rest of the way to Curl Lake. Along the way lies one of the Broadwater Meadow Lakes, essentially a scenic wide spot in the stream.

Stay alert at the head of Broadwater Meadow Lake. Just past this point, the trail gets more difficult to find, especially just before Curl Lake. The shoreline of Curl Lake is steep and rocky, but there are places to camp.

> **Fishing information:** The Broadwater River provides a beautiful setting to fish a mountain stream. The Broadwater Meadow Lakes are known for their brook trout, providing a good opportunity to work on fly casting. Curl and Broadwater lakes are both brook trout fisheries.
>
> A side trip can be made cross-country east, through the burned area, to Sedge and Dollar lakes to fish grayling. Cutthroat trout have migrated downstream to these lakes and are out-competing the grayling for space, so this precious fishery may eventually be lost.

43 *LAKE VERNON*

General description: An easy day hike.
Total distance: 5 miles.
Difficulty: Easy.
Topo maps: USGS—Fossil Lake; RMS—Cooke City-Cutoff Mountain.

Key points:

0.5 Junction with Kersey Lake Jeep Road.
1.2 Junction with Lake Vernon Trail 565.
1.8 Lillis Lake.

LAKE VERNON

The trail: Lake Vernon is a great choice for a day hike with small children. The trail is well-maintained and easy to follow all the way. It passes through a rich, unburned forest, and there are no major hills. Keep a sharp eye out for moose, especially in the big meadow just before Lillis Lake.

The trail doesn't have abundant drinking water, so bring an extra bottle. Like all trails in this area, mosquitoes can be bothersome, especially early in the summer.

To reach Lake Vernon, take Trail 3 from the Clarks Fork Trailhead for about 1.2 miles to a well-signed junction with Trail 564 to Lake Vernon. Turn right (south) and head up a moderate grade. After another 0.5 mile or so look for little, jewel-like Lillis Lake in the foreground with majestic Pilot Peak and Index Peak as a backdrop.

The trail continues around the northwest shoreline of Lillis Lake less than a mile more to the destination, Lake Vernon. This forest-lined lake is larger than Lillis but offers a

Lake Vernon.

similar view of Pilot and Index. Just south of Lake Vernon is Lower Lake Vernon, more appropriately called Reed Lake on some maps since it's little more than a scenic marsh.

Although better suited for day hiking, Lake Vernon also has a few campsites. Perhaps the best campsite is on the left just before the trail hits the lake.

On the way out of Lake Vernon, the trail climbs the biggest hill of the trip, about 0.5 mile long. Once at the top, however, it's downhill all the way to the trailhead.

➤ **Fishing information:** This short day hike offers some surprising fishing. Brook trout have trouble reproducing in Lillis Lake, and the smaller population translates into bigger brookies. Be sure to stop at this small lake on the way to Vernon, which hosts both cutthroat and brook trout. Just over the hill, you could find yourself alone catching stocked cutthroats at Margaret Lake.

44 ROCK ISLAND LAKE

General description: An easy day hike or overnighter.
Total distance: 6 miles.
Difficulty: Easy.
Topo maps: USGS—Fossil Lake; RMS—Cooke City-Cutoff Mountain.

Key points:

0.5   Junction with Kersey Lake Jeep Road.
1.2   Junction with Trail 565 to Lake Vernon.
1.5   Kersey Lake.
2.4   Junction with Trail 565 to Rock Island Lake.
3.0   Rock Island Lake.

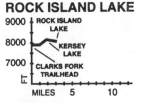

ROCK ISLAND LAKE

The trail: Rock Island Lake differs from many high-elevation lakes. Instead of forming a small, concise oval in the end of a cirque, it sprawls through flat and forested terrain, seemingly branching off in every direction. Visitors can spend an entire day just walking around it.

To get to Rock Island Lake, take Trail 3 from the Clarks Fork Trailhead to the junction with Trail 565 to Rock Island Lake. Turn right (east) here for about another 0.5 mile to the lake. The trail is well-used and well-maintained the entire way with only one hill (near Kersey Lake). The 1988 fires scorched the area around Kersey Lake but missed Rock Island Lake.

Those planning an overnight stay can camp at one of several places along the west side of the lake. However, camping spots are more limited than many other lakes in the Beartooths, and you might have to search awhile to find an unoccupied spot.

Because Rock Island Lake is so accessible and easy to reach (3 miles on a near-level trail), it's a perfect choice for a family planning their first trip into the Absaroka-Beartooth Wilderness. Drinking water is readily available on the trail and at the lake

Rock Island Lake with Pilot Peak and Index Peak in the background.

(it must be boiled or filtered), but the mosquitoes are bad in early summer. Although there might be enough wood for a campfire at the lake, consider using a stove for cooking. The area receives heavy use, and if everyone had a fire, the area would soon show signs of overuse.

> | **Fishing information:** This popular lake has a combination of home-grown brookies and cutthroats stocked on a three-year rotation, both of which grow well in this lake. The fishing should generally be good enough to count on for dinner.

45 FOX LAKE

General description: A moderately easy overnighter.
Total distance: 8 miles.
Difficulty: Moderate.
Topo maps: USGS—Fossil Lake; RMS—Cooke City-Cutoff Mountain.

Key points:

0.5   Junction with Kersey Lake Jeep Road.
1.2   Junction with Trail 565 to Lake Vernon.
1.5   Kersey Lake.
2.4   Junction with Trail 565 to Rock Island Lake.
2.6   Junction with Trail 567 to Russell Lake.
3.6   Junction with trail down to Fox Lake.

FOX LAKE

The trail: Fox Lake is the first of a long chain of lakes called Crazy Lakes, and it's a good choice for a moderate overnight trip.

To get to Fox Lake, take Trail 3 from the Clarks Fork Trailhead. The trail passes through mostly unburned forest (except for a section by Kersey Lake) for about 3.6 miles. Then look for a trail heading right (southeast) to Fox Lake. Be careful not to take two earlier right hand turns to Rock Island Lake or Crazy Lakes.

The trail climbs gradually as it heads toward the high plateau. The turn onto the Fox Lake trail leads to a steep, 0.5-mile downhill to the lake.

Fox Lake is large and striking. Explorers can follow the shoreline around to the right (west), but not to the left where steep climbs jut up from the lake.

There's a large camping area on the west side of where Russell Creek slips into Fox Lake. This is the only campsite, but it's suitable for a large party or more than one small group. The site is not suited for backcountry horsemen. Farley Creek also tumbles into Fox Lake just to the east of Russell Creek. These two streams merge in Fox Lake and leave the lake as Crazy Creek.

For a fairly rough side trip, follow a crude angler's trail up Farley Creek to Canyon Lake. This is a steep, difficult-to-follow trail.

On the way out of Fox Lake, be prepared to climb that major hill you came down on the way in. But from that point, it's downhill to the trailhead except for a short slope along Kersey Lake.

➤ | **Fishing information:** Fox Lake is a personal favorite, although close to the trailhead. Most day hikers stop at Kersey or head over to Rock Island. Overnighters generally pass on by on The Beaten Path. Fox has oversized brookies, nice rainbows, and an occasional grayling that slipped down from Cliff Lake. Cliff Lake is a worthwhile side trip for the hearty (no trail). It has an abundance of 8-to 12-inch grayling.

TRAILHEAD 15

FISHER CREEK

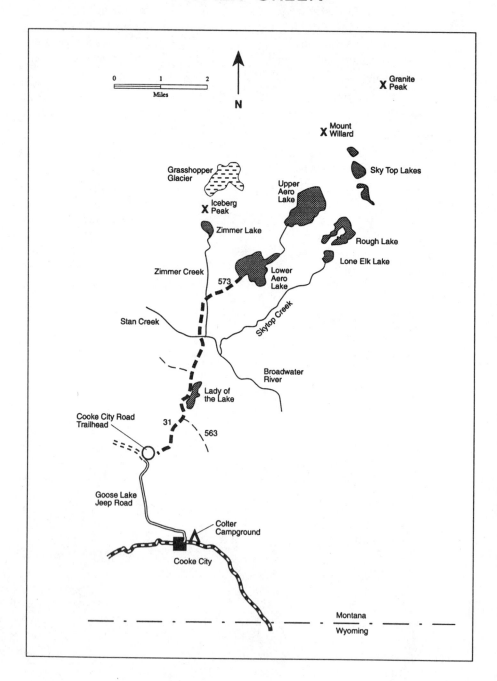

0 1 2
Miles

N

X Granite Peak

X Mount Willard

Grasshopper Glacier

Sky Top Lakes

X Iceberg Peak

Upper Aero Lake

Zimmer Lake

Zimmer Creek

Rough Lake

Lone Elk Lake

573

Lower Aero Lake

Stan Creek

Skytop Creek

Broadwater River

Lady of the Lake

Cooke City Road Trailhead

31

563

Goose Lake Jeep Road

Colter Campground

Cooke City

Montana

Wyoming

OVERVIEW

This trailhead is slightly harder to locate than most others in the Beartooths, but this hasn't lessened its popularity. The area has lots to offer, and it receives heavy use both by locals and those who travel from afar for a chance to experience this spectacular wild area.

One of the best short, easy trips (Lady of the Lake) in the Beartooths begins here, as does one of the most popular wilderness adventures (the Aero Lakes area).

The trailhead lies on the eastern fringe of the section of the Beartooths that has been extensively mined, logged, and roaded. Even in the 2 miles of gravel road to the trailhead, the contrast between this area and the pristine wilderness is clearly evident.

Camp at the undeveloped campground at the trailhead to get an earlier start, a particularly good idea for those headed into Aero Lakes.

FINDING THE TRAILHEAD

To reach the trailhead from Cooke City, drive east on U.S. Highway 212 for 3.2 miles to a turnoff marked with a large Forest Service sign as the Goose Lake Jeep Road, just before the Colter Campground. Turn north off U.S. Highway 212 and drive northeast about 2 miles up this gravel road to a cluster of old buildings. An inconspicuous trailhead on the right shoulder of the road has an old Forest Service sign for Lady of the Lake. The 2 miles of road to the trailhead are passable with any vehicle, but to continue up the road past the trailhead for any reason a high-clearance vehicle is essential.

THE TRAILS

Lady of the Lake
Aero Lakes Base Camp

46 LADY OF THE LAKE

General description: An easy day hike or overnighter.
Total distance: 3 miles.
Difficulty: Easy.
Special attractions: A gorgeous and accessible forested lake.
Topo maps: USGS—Cooke City; RMS—Cooke City-Cutoff Mountain.

The trail: Lady of the Lake is an ideal choice for an easy day hike or overnighter with small children. Besides being a short hike, the weather isn't as critical as it is at the higher elevations.

Unfortunately, hikers might have to get their feet wet imme-

LADY OF THE LAKE

9000

8000

LADY OF THE LAKE

MILES   5

diately upon starting this trip. The bridge over Fisher Creek washed out years ago, and until late in the year, the stream carries too much water to ford without wading.

After Fisher Creek, the trail goes by a small private inholding with a cabin, and then heads down a well-maintained, forest-lined trail to Lady of the Lake. The Forest Service sign says 1 mile to the lake, but it's probably more like 1.5 miles. The trail breaks out of the trees in the large marshy meadow at the foot of the lake.

Just before the lake, Trail 563 heads off to the right (south) to Chief Joseph Campground on US 212. Trail 563 also offers fairly easy access to Lady of the Lake, but the route described here is much shorter and faster.

This is a heavily used area, with some major wear and tear along the trail on the west shore of the lake. The Forest Service has prohibited camping at several overused sites to allow rehabilitation. For overnighters, the best campsite is about halfway along the lake on the left just after a cut in a huge log across the trail and through a small meadow. Campfires are allowed.

The return trip involves more climbing than the way in, so allow extra time, especially if traveling with small children.

➤ | **Fishing information:** Lady of the Lake is a personal favorite of places to take kids for their first wilderness camping experience. The hike is easy, and the brook trout are always willing. For those with some wilderness experience, there are four small lakes nestled in the trees to the southeast. They're a bit tough to find, but they promise solitude. Grayling are stocked in Mosquito Lake when available, while the other lakes are scheduled for stocking with cutthroats.

Don't bother to fish Fisher Creek. Acid effluent from mines abandoned before environmental protection laws were in place keeps this stream pretty sterile.

47 AERO LAKES BASE CAMP

General description:	A strenuous base-camp trip into the heart of the Beartooth's alpine country.
Total distance:	12 miles, not counting side trips.
Difficulty:	Difficult.
Special attractions:	The stark beauty of this high plateau area.
Topo maps:	USGS—Cooke City, Fossil Lake, and Granite Peak; RMS—Cooke-City-Cutoff Mountain.

Upper Aero Lake, the second deepest in the Beartooths.

Key points:

1.5	Lady of the Lake.
2.5	Junction with trail to Long Lake.
2.8	Stream coming in from Long Lake.
3.6	Star Creek.
4.8	Start of climb to Aero Lakes.
5.7	Lower Aero Lake.

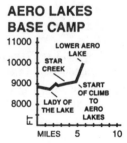

**AERO LAKES
BASE CAMP**

The trail: At Aero Lakes, you're many miles from the nearest machine. At night, no city lights or smog block the view of the stars. Nearly one million acres of pristine land surrounds you here, more than enough for a lifetime of wandering.

At this altitude, the summer season is very short. Ice may not free the lakes until mid-July. The moist tundra tends to produce a prodigious number of mosquitoes when the wind isn't blowing. Bring lots of bug dope.

To get to Aero Lakes, take the same route described earlier to Lady of the Lake. Once at Lady of the Lake follow the trail along the west side of the lake. At the far end of the lake, the trail heads off to the left for about 0.25 mile to a meadow on the north side of the lake where two trails depart. The left trail heads northwest to Long Lake. Take the right trail, which leads almost due north less than 0.5 mile to the confluence of Star and Zimmer creeks. Ford the stream here and continue north along Zimmer Creek another mile or so until you see Trail 573 switchbacking up the steep right side of the cirque. If you see a major stream coming in from the left, you have gone too

Rough Lake, perhaps named for its environment.

far up the drainage.

The scramble up the switchbacks is short but steep and requires good physical conditioning. The locals have an excellent reason for calling this "Cardiac Hill."

At the top of Cardiac Hill, the trail suddenly emerges from the timber and pauses above Lower Aero Lake. Be sure to notice the dramatic contrast between the treeless plateau here and the timbered country below.

The shoreline around Lower Aero is rocky and punctuated with snowbanks. There are a number of places to camp. They all have great scenery, and the air conditioning is always on. Those planning to stay here for two or three nights should spend some extra time searching for that five-star campsite. Drop the packs and look around for an hour or so. Don't expect to have a campfire on this treeless plateau. Perhaps the best campsite at Lower Aero is on the grassy north side where a point juts out into the lake.

To proceed to Upper Aero Lake, follow the stream that connects the two lakes. Another good camping spot is just below the outlet of the upper lake. This provides a good view of the lake and prominent Mount Villard with its spiny ridges. It also makes a good base camp for fishing both lakes and for exploring east to Rough Lake and then north up the Sky Top Lakes chain.

Although most people visit Rough Lake or Lone Elk Lake on side trips, there's also good camping there. Both are large, deep lakes similar to Aero Lakes. Sky Top Lakes might look inviting on the map, but camping is very limited in this rocky basin.

After a day or two of exploring the high country, either retrace your steps down Cardiac Hill to Zimmer Creek or make a loop out of the trip by going down Sky Top Creek from Lone Elk Lake. Be forewarned: this route is only for the fit, agile, and adventuresome.

First of all, it requires carrying your pack cross-country over to Rough Lake (probably named for how hard it is to reach) and then down to Lone Elk Lake. From Lone Elk Lake, it's a scramble down a steep route with no trail to a meadow where the stream from Splinter Lake slips into Sky Top Creek. This is a long, slow mile, and it can be hazardous, so be careful and patient. But it's also very beautiful, especially the falls where Sky Top Creek leaves Lone Elk Lake.

Once at the meadow, there is an unofficial trail along Sky Top Creek all the way to the main trail. Follow cascading Sky Top Creek all the way until near the end when it veers off to the left to join up with Star Creek to form the Broadwater River. The track comes out into the same meadow (where Star and Zimmer creeks join) you passed through on the way up Zimmer Creek on Trail 573. From here, retrace your steps back to Lady of the Lake and the trailhead.

WHERE TO GO FROM AERO LAKES

While in the Aero Lakes area set aside a day or two for exploring the "top of the world." Day trips in this area are generally more advanced than in other parts of the Beartooths. Here's a list of suggestions rated for difficulty as follows: "Human" (easy for almost everyone, including children), "Semi-Human" (moderately difficult), or "Animal" (don't try it unless you're very fit and wilderness-wise). Also refer to more detailed rating information in the chapter, "Using this Guidebook."

Destination	Difficulty
Aero Lakes perimeter	Semi-Human
Upper Aero Lake	Human
Leaky Raft Lake	Human
Rough Lake	Semi-Human
Lone Elk Lake	Semi-Human
Sky Top Lakes	Animal
Zimmer Lake	Animal
Iceberg Peak & Grasshopper Glacier	Animal
Mount Villard	Animal
Glacier Peak	Animal

Fishing information: Fishing is generally slow in both Upper and Lower Aero Lakes, but the rewards can be worth it. Lower Aero has brookies that are large, occasionally approaching a pound or more. This is supplemented with cutthroats that have migrated down from Upper Aero and seem to be reproducing. Cutts can be seen trying to spawn between the lakes through most of July. Upper Aero is stocked with cutts, but a change in its current six-year cycle is being discussed. Fishing is tough here as the cutthroats tend to school, and they can be hard to find in a lake of this size.

Sky Top Lakes were once stocked with grayling, and these worked down into Rough and Lone Elk lakes, but all seem to have disappeared, leaving just brook trout in Lone Elk and Rough. The Sky Tops will probably be stocked once again to maintain a fishery in this chain originating on the slopes of Granite Peak.

To the east of Sky Top Creek are a number of lakes, supporting mostly brook trout, although Weasel, Stash, and Surprise lakes are stocked with cutts. For hearty souls, Recruitment Lake holds a few extremely large brookies, but the chances of getting skunked are pretty good. Nevertheless, just one hefty fish from this lake would be the high point of a summer vacation.

Rugged Sky Top Lakes.

TRAILHEAD 16
LAKE ABUNDANCE

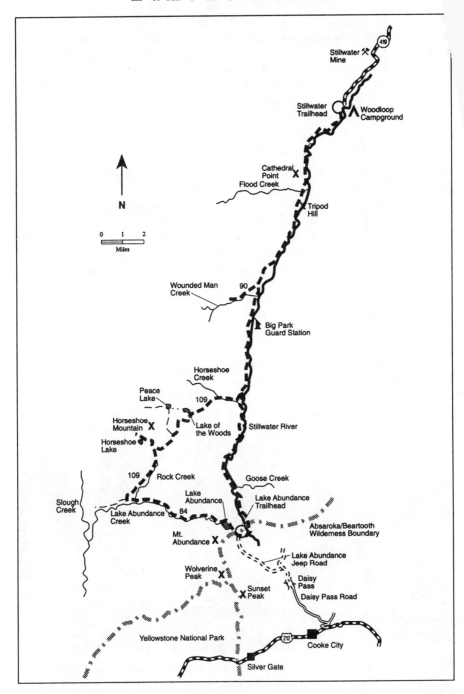

e Lake Abundance Trailhead offers a great opportunity to see the al-
vilderness.

north of Cooke City is heavily mineralized and has been mined since the
century. And it still shows it. Even after decades, nature has not come close
ing this fragile, high-altitude region. Imagine what this area used to be like,
he 19th century. Also, use your imagination to picture what might happen
rrently proposed, more large mining developments open up in this area.

ure, however, does have one trick left. In winter, heavy snows cover all signs
past, and the area becomes de facto wilderness. Winter use—snowmobiling
cross-country skiing—is quite popular in this area.

INDING THE TRAILHEAD

Most trailheads in the Beartooths are quite accessible. This one is the other extreme.
Just getting here can be quite the experience.

The road to Daisy Pass leaves U.S. Highway 212 virtually on the easternmost city
limits of Cooke City. It's about 8 miles to the trailhead.

The first 4 miles are on a well-maintained gravel road that can be traversed by
any two-wheel-drive vehicle. About 0.5 mile after the top of Daisy Pass, turn left
(west) on the Lake Abundance Jeep Road, which is not maintained. From this point
on, don't proceed with anything less than a high-clearance, four-wheel-drive vehicle
and several seasons of serious four-wheeling experience. There is camping at an undeveloped campground at the trailhead.

The Lake Abundance Trailhead, the most remote and inaccessible in the Beartooths.

48 *LAKE ABUNDANCE LOOP*

General description: A long and difficult loop through some of the most re-
mote and untamed country left in the continental
United States.
Total distance: 29 miles.
Difficulty: Very difficult and demanding, strictly for the experi-
enced and skilled wilderness travelers only.
Special attractions: The wildest, most remote trip in this book.
Topo maps: USGS—Cooke City, Cutoff Mountain, Little Park
Mountain, and Pinnacle Mountain; RMS—Cooke City-
Cutoff Mountain.

Key points:

2.1 Goose Creek.
9.6 Junction with Horseshoe Creek Trail 34.
15.9 Junction with Trail 109.
16.0 Lake of the Woods.
16.5 Junction with Trail 109.
18.5 Trail to Horseshoe Lake.
21.2 Junction with Lake Abundance Trail 84.
27.7 Lake Abundance.
28.7 Lake Abundance Trailhead.

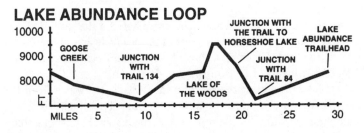

The trail: This trip is not for the beginner or the faint-hearted. It goes through the
wildest, most isolated country in the Beartooths, and most of the trail is poorly
maintained and, in places, hard to find. Be sure to allow extra travel time for covering rough ground and route-finding.

On the plus side, travelers here will think they have the entire universe to themselves because the area receives so little use. In this realm of solitude and untamed

grandeur, you become immersed in the true spirit of the wilderness.

From the trailhead head down Stillwater River Trail 24, which takes off just across the little stream meandering through a large high-altitude meadow just east of the trailhead. This is the headwaters of the Stillwater River, though it doesn't look like much of a river at this point. That changes about 2 miles downstream when Goose Creek joins the upper Stillwater.

After a pleasant 0.5-mile walk through the flat meadow, the trail drops over the end of the plateau and starts a steep downhill grade along the still small Stillwater River. When Goose Creek cascades in from the east, the gradient flattens out a bit and grows steadily more gradual all the way to the junction with Trail 34 up Horseshoe Creek. Cross the Stillwater where Goose Creek comes in—there's no bridge. It's safe to cross here, but plan on getting wet feet.

The first 4 miles of trail traverse a somewhat stark landscape, carpeted with flat, glaciated rock and punctuated like a pin cushion with whitish snags. It was semistark before the fires of 1988, but one of the burns scorched its way down the Stillwater to finish the job. It's a lonely, cheerless stretch.

But then the landscape becomes more diverse and moist, supporting abundant wildlife populations, especially elk and deer. You should start looking for the first night's campsite somewhere along this reach of the upper Stillwater. There's no shortage of agreeable sites, so where to stop depends more on how far you want to go on the first day in.

A little more than 9 miles into the trek, start watching for the turn off to Horseshoe Creek. This junction is easy to miss, and it could be a long detour if you miss it. Refer to a topo map frequently to be sure you've crossed Horseshoe Creek. Shortly after the stream crossing, Trail 34 heads west out of a small meadow. There probably won't be a sign, but look for the post that once held the sign. The grassy meadow also tends to swallow up the trail as it departs, but attentive hikers won't miss it. After the first 50 yards, the trail becomes easy to follow, although from here on out the trail has received little trail maintenance.

Trail 34 climbs moderately to Lake of the Woods, following the creek all the way. About 1 mile before Lake of the Woods, the trail breaks out into a scenic subalpine landscape that burned only in spots. Lake of the Woods is a shallow pristine lake surrounded by marshy meadows. Those who camp here for the second night should set aside some time for the short side trip over to Peace Lake and, if there's time and energy to spare, the bushwhack up a short, 600-foot climb to Heather Lake, which is about 2 miles northwest of Lake of the Woods.

About 100 feet before hitting the shoreline at Lake of the Woods, Trail 109 takes off to the south. This junction can be difficult to find; backtrack from the lake if necessary and look carefully for the trail as it starts to switchback up a steep grade to the south. Again, the trail is easy to follow after the first 100 yards.

After the tough but short climb (gaining about 900 feet), the trail breaks out above timberline at 9,500 feet and follows a narrow ridge for a while. Set an easy pace and soak in the great scenery. Look west to 10,111-foot Horseshoe Mountain, north to 10,272-foot Timberline Mountain, and 8 miles south to 10,500-foot Wolverine Peak on the northwest boundary of Yellowstone National Park. As the trail drops off the ridge, keep the topo map and compass out—the trail fades away in several places.

If you plan on spending four nights out, camp at Horseshoe Lake for the third night. If you're out for only three nights, it might be wise to forge on to Lake Abundance Creek and camp there. Horseshoe Lake still bears a few signs of early century mining activity around its shores.

From Horseshoe Basin, descend gradually toward Lake Abundance Creek, following Rock Creek most of the way. This area escaped the 1988 fires and is loaded with wildlife, including a healthy bear population, so stay alert.

About 3 miles from Horseshoe Basin, turn left (east) on Trail 84 at the only easy-to-find junction on this trip. Then follow Lake Abundance Creek all the way back to the trailhead, about 7.5 miles total. This drainage is moist and lush, excellent wildlife habitat. The trail is poorly maintained, so plan on climbing over a few downed trees. The trail skirts the north shore of Lake Abundance for about half of the final mile to the trailhead.

➤ **Fishing information:** For anglers, the highlight of this trip is the possibility of catching aboriginal Yellowstone cutthroat trout strain. Peace and Heather lakes have never been stocked and contain original cutthroats. It seems that someone took a few of these over the pass and placed them in Lake of the Woods, as the same stock is found there. While none of these fish are large, just catching them may be satisfying.

The entire Slough Creek drainage supports only cutthroats. Stocking of Yellowstone cutthroats has occurred in many places, including the creek itself. Currently only Lake Abundance (on a three-year cycle) and Horseshoe Lake (on an eight-year cycle) are stocked. Fish grow exceptionally well in Lake Abundance, and it's certainly worth the stop.

49 THE COMPLETE STILLWATER

General description: A trans-Beartooth shuttle, following the Stillwater River all the way.
Total distance: 28 miles.
Difficulty: Moderate, but long.
Topo maps: USGS—Cooke City, Cutoff Mountain, Little Park Mountain, Pinnacle Mountain, and Cathedral Point; RMS—Cooke City-Cutoff Mountain and Mount Douglas-Mount Wood.

Key points:

- 2.1 Goose Creek.
- 9.6 Junction with Horseshoe Creek Trail 34.
- 14.9 Big Park Guard Station.
- 16.6 Wounded Man Creek.
- 16.8 Junction with West Stillwater Trail 90.
- 21.6 Tripod Hill.
- 22.3 Flood Creek.
- 24.8 Sioux Charley Lake.
- 27.8 Stillwater River Trailhead.

THE COMPLETE STILLWATER

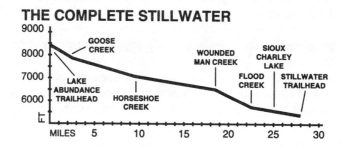

The Upper Stillwater, just before it begins its long, steep plunge to the north edge of the Beartooths. Michael S. Sample photo.

The trail: This trip can be traveled from either end, of course, but most people will prefer starting at Lake Abundance because, quite frankly, it's easier. In fact, it's downhill all the way. There aren't many trails where hikers can go 28 miles without a single uphill pitch.

Try to arrange for somebody to drop you off at Lake Abundance and then leave a vehicle or arrange for a pick-up at the Stillwater River Trailhead. The "trading keys" option doesn't work well on this trail because one party has to agree to walk 28 miles uphill so the other group gets 28 miles downhill. Arranging the shuttle may be a hassle, but it allows the rare chance to travel all the way through the Beartooths along the Stillwater River. There are only two other ways to traverse the entire area and stay on established trails. These are "The Beaten Path" trail up the East Rosebud, and the East Boulder/Slough Creek trip going from the Boulder down into Yellowstone Park.

From the marvelous, high-mountain park at the trailhead, this trail travels through 28 miles of forested river valley. The 1988 fires burned through the Stillwater, and the first 4 miles still show the results. But now the forest is springing back, and the entire area is lush and full of wildlife.

To some, the prospect of traveling 28 miles through one continuous valley forest might sound monotonous. And granted, this route offers none of the thrills of "bagging" a major peak or watching sunsets burnish the surface of some icy alpine tarn. But it more than makes up for this by immersing the traveler in remote wilderness, in a place at once peaceful and refreshing.

The trail is in good shape all the way and is well traveled north of the junction with Wounded Man Creek and Trail 90. Potential campsites are abundant along the entire route, and there is plenty of wood for thought-provoking campfires.

For descriptions of the route, refer to the "Stillwater to Stillwater" trip listed under the West Stillwater trailhead, and the "Lake Abundance Loop" trip at the beginning of this section.

Be sure to take the time for the short side trip over to Tripod Hill at mile 21.6. There's an obvious trail going east just before the Flood Creek bridge. The point provides a spectacular view of the Stillwater River drainage, including well-named Cathedral Point to the south just past Flood Creek. At Flood Creek, a glance at the map shows that it isn't far to Flood Creek Falls. But this is an extremely difficult bushwhack, which is really too bad because Flood Creek Falls is one of the most spectacular sights in the Beartooths and one that very few people will ever see.

Fishing information: The Stillwater above Goose Creek doesn't support a fishery and probably never has. The steep cascades block upstream migration. Fish begin to appear in the river at Goose Creek; below here there are brook trout as well as rainbows and cutthroat. The farther downstream you go, the better the fishing.

Keep in mind, as you fish, that the steeper the terrain, the less hospitable it is for trout. Look for fish in the slower water. Rainbows and cutthroats are slightly more suited to faster, colder water, and they do better than brookies in the fast places.

Most anglers agree that brook trout are the best eating of the three types of trout found here, and eating them will only help the remaining fish to grow bigger. Plan on taking a meal with you as you leave; there will be plenty left for those who follow.

Sioux Charley Lake is really just a wide, slow spot in the river where many people choose to stop.

EPILOGUE

A BAD IDEA?

It has been whispered here and there that books like this are a bad idea.

The theory goes something like this: Guidebooks bring more people into the wilderness; more people cause more environmental damage; and the wildness we all seek gradually evaporates.

I used to think like that, too. And here's why I changed my mind.

When I wrote and published my first guidebook in 1979 (*The Hiker's Guide to Montana*), some of my hiking buddies disapproved. Since then, I've published more than 35 hiking and trail guides, and I'm proud of it.

I also hope these books have increased wilderness use.

Experienced hikers tend to have a lofty attitude toward the inexperienced masses. They think anybody who wants to backpack can buy a topo map and compass and find their own way through the wilderness. But the fact is, most people want a guide. Sometimes, the inexperienced hikers prefer a real, live person to show them the way and help them build confidence, but most of the time, they can get by with a trail guide like this one.

All guidebooks published by Falcon (and most published by other publishers) invite wilderness users to respect and support the protection of wild country. Sometimes this is direct editorializing. Sometimes this invitation takes the more subtle form of simply helping people experience wilderness. And it's a rare person who leaves a place like the Beartooths without a firmly planted passion for wild country. Anybody who has spent a few nights in nature's penthouse is going to want more wilderness.

In classes on backpacking taught for the Yellowstone Institute, I have taken hundreds of people into the wilderness. Many of them had a backpack on for the first time. Many of them were not convinced that we need more wilderness, but they were all convinced when they arrived back at the trailhead. Many, many times, I've seen it happen without saying a single word about wilderness.

It doesn't take preaching. Instead, we just need to get people out into the wilderness where the essence of wildness sort of sneaks up on your heart and takes root, and before you know it, it's too late.

But what about overcrowding? Yes, it's a problem in many places and probably will be in the Beartooths. The answer to overused wilderness is not limiting use of wilderness and restrictive regulations. The answer is more wilderness.

How can we convince people to support more wilderness when they have never experienced wilderness? In my opinion, we can't.

As a volunteer board member of the Montana Wilderness Association, I worked hard to convince Congress to designate the Absaroka-Beartooth Wilderness. During that struggle, I often thought that if we had a letter of support from everybody who hiked into the Beartooths from the East Rosebud or at Island Lake, we would have had an easier fight.

That's why we need guidebooks. And that's why I changed my mind. Now, I believe guidebooks have done as much to build support for wilderness as pro-wilderness organizations have ever done through political and public relation efforts.

And if that's not enough, here's another reason. All FalconGuides (and most guidebooks published by other publishers) contain sections on no-trace camping and wilderness safety. Guidebooks provide a perfect medium for communicating this vital information to the inexperienced.

In 30 years of backpacking, I have seen dramatic changes in how backpackers care for wilderness. I've seen it go from appalling to exceptional. Today, almost everybody walks softly in the wilderness. And I believe the information contained in guidebooks has been partly responsible for this change.

Having said all that, I hope many thousands of people use this book to enjoy a fun-filled vacation amid the breathtaking beauty and deafening quiet of the Beartooths—and then, of course, vote for wilderness preservation for the rest of their lives.

—Bill Schneider, Publisher

BRING ALONG A COMPANION

On your next trip to the great outdoors, bring along *Wild Country Companion*. This new FalconGuide includes state-of-the-art methods for safe, no-trace traveling in North America's backcountry. Whether you're on foot, horse or bike, this book offers new ways to sustain our outdoor recreation resources.

Wild Country Companion
By Will Harmon
Illustrated by Lisa Harvey
160 pp., 6 x 9", charts, softcover.

For more information on this and other Falcon Press books visit your local bookstore. Or call 1-800-582-2665

ABOUT THE AUTHOR

LIVING LIFE ONE MILE AT A TIME

Contrary to rumors, Wild Bill Lake was not named for the author.

Whenever Bill Schneider isn't out in the wilderness, he wants to be. He has spent more than 30 years hiking Montana trails.

In the beginning, during college in the late 1960s, he worked on a trail crew in Glacier National Park. Then he spent the 1970s publishing the *Montana Outdoors Magazine* for the Montana Department of Fish, Wildlife and Parks and covering as many miles of trails as possible on weekends and holidays.

In 1979, Bill, along with his business partner to this day, Mike Sample, established Falcon Press Publishing and published two guidebooks the first year. Bill wrote one of them, *The Hiker's Guide to Montana,* now titled *Hiking Montana,* which is still a popular guidebook. He has also written four other books and many magazine articles on wildlife, outdoor recreation, and environmental issues. Along the way, on a part-time basis over a span of 12 years, Bill has taught classes on bicycling, backpacking, no-trace camping, and hiking in bear country for The Yellowstone Institute, a nonprofit educational organization in Yellowstone National Park.

Since 1979 Bill has served as publisher of Falcon Press which is now established as a premier publisher of recreational guidebooks with more than 200 titles in print.